Hungry Girl

Hungry Girl

Recipes and Survival Strategies for Guilt-Free Eating in the Real World

Lisa Lillien

St. Martin's Griffin
New York

HUNGRY GIRL: RECIPES AND SURVIVAL STRATEGIES FOR GUILT-FREE EATING IN THE REAL WORLD. Copyright © 2008 by Hungry Girl, Inc. All rights reserved. Printed in the United States of America. No part of this book may be used or reproduced in any manner whatsoever without written permission except in the case of brief quotations embodied in critical articles or reviews. For information, address St. Martin's Press, 175 Fifth Avenue, New York, N.Y. 10010.

www.stmartins.com

Cover design and book design by Elizabeth Hodson

Illustrations by Jack Pullan

Food styling and photography by Kelly Cline

Library of Congress Cataloging-in-Publication Data Available Upon Request

ISBN-13: 978-0-312-37742-7

ISBN-10: 0-312-37742-8

10 9 8 7 6

This book is dedicated to all the Hungry Girl subscribers. Your devotion and loyalty are appreciated and valued more than you will ever know.

Contents

Acknowledgments

The inspiration for Hungry Girl came to me in 2003 as I was speeding down the freeway with a car full of desserts I was taking to a laboratory to be tested for nutritional information. The pastries came from a local bakery, and I was obsessed with them because they were fantastic and (supposedly) very low-calorie. But they were just a little *too* good. I was suspicious. As I zoomed along, it occurred to me that my bizarre passion for guilt-free foods could somehow help the world. So I quit my cushy job and started a free daily email subscription service called Hungry Girl. The first HG email went out to less than 100 people, mostly friends. Today, Hungry Girl has over 400,000 subscribers. (P.S. The lab confirmed my suspicions—those pastries had WAY more calories than the bakery claimed.)

I am the founder and voice of Hungry Girl, but running a company that churns out so much content isn't something I could ever do alone. This book is the result of countless hours of hard work by a very small yet amazing group of people. And they all deserve to share the credit for it with me.

Elizabeth Hodson, thank you for being with me since Day One, back when we had only seventy-eight subscribers (aka, our friends and families). You've always given a billion percent of yourself to Hungry Girl. Everything you design looks sooooo awesome and cute (including this book)! I'm also convinced that you and I share the same taste buds, which I value even more than you know. Please, PLEASE work with me forever.

Jamie Goldberg, I love your feisty passion for detail, and your obsession with grammar and all things guilt-free. It's obvious that Hungry Girl is much more to you than just a job. Thank you for putting your blood, sweat, tears, and tongue into this book and never giving up when you believe in something. Please keep on challenging me because this book wouldn't be the same without you.

Lynn Bettencourt, thanks for putting up with me, for lugging hundreds of food-filled boxes up countless steps, and for all that Turkey Taco Meatloaf (see page 132). You wear a lot of hats at HG headquarters, and you wear them all well (especially your Red Sox hat!).

Alison Kreuch, I swear, you have the energy of nine nuclear power plants! It's because of you that HG can pay its bills. I'd run Hungry Girl for free (seriously), but thanks to you, we don't have to.

John Vaccaro, you're a guy, but you'll always be an honorary Hungry Girl—even though you order two entrees at a time (and usually fatty ones) and I know you'd never eat anything I cook or write about. Your expertise in PowerPoint and Excel makes your greasy-food consumption 100 percent excusable.

Tom Fineman, you put the "pro" in "bono" (yes, I know that makes no sense). You're the best entertainment lawyer in Los Angeles—and perhaps even the tallest! I'm so lucky to have you on the HG team. I'd say you're a great friend, but you're really more like family.

Neeti Madan, you are a superhero and *literally* (get it???), the best agent a hungry girl could ever have. Thanks a million times over.

Jennifer Enderlin and **Matthew Shear,** thank you both for believing in Hungry Girl, for trusting me, for publishing this book, and for making the whole process more fun than I ever could've imagined. Everyone's "first time" should be with you guys (don't take that the wrong way!).

To **Lisa Senz, John Murphy, John Karle,** and the amazing marketing and PR crews over at St. Martin's—thankyouthankyouthankyou!

Special thanks to **Jennifer Curtis, Ina Burke, Jackie MacDougall, Dena Krischer, Jack Pullan,** and **Lorig Koujakian.** All of you made invaluable contributions to this book. Let's do more fun HG projects together in the future!

To my parents, **Florence and Maurice Lillien,** I may have conceived Hungry Girl, but you conceived me (nice work, guys!). Thank you for your neverending love and support. To my sister, **Meri Lillien,** a great friend and the ultimate super-sleuth, who can sniff out guilt-free finds as well as anyone I know. And to my brother, **Jay Lillien,** who I've always secretly envied for his ability to eat an entire box of Lucky Charms (with whole milk!) in one sitting and not gain an ounce.

To **Cookie** and **Jackson,** my furry babies who keep me sane and calm when life gets crazy. And to sweet **Mischief,** who is no longer with us, but was a major part of Hungry Girl (not to mention a huge fan of Fiber One) from the very beginning.

To the love of my life, my husband, best friend, and partner, **Daniel Schneider.** Your insight and brilliance inspire me every day. Thank you for your endless creativity, for loving me unconditionally, and making me laugh harder than I've ever laughed before. You are the reason Hungry Girl exists.

Hungry Girl

Introduction

FAQs (Frequently Asked Questions)

Who/What is Hungry Girl?

If you're holding this book in your hands, there's a good chance you already know the answer to this question. But for those of you who don't know, Hungry Girl is a free daily email about guilt-free eating. Our news, food finds, recipes, and survival strategies are read by hundreds of thousands of people every day. To sign up or see all of our past content, go to Hungry-Girl.com.

Is Hungry Girl a real person? And is she a doctor?

Yes, I'm a real person. I'm Lisa Lillien, and I'm not a nutritionist or a doctor. I'm just hungry, and a bit obsessed with foods that taste great but don't pack on the pounds. I'm the nut who watches you shop at the supermarket, comments on your choice of low-fat ice cream, and tells you which brand to buy (FYI, Dreyer's/Edy's Slow Churned is the way to go). HG's daily emails and all other HG content are the result of extensive research done by me and my super-dedicated and talented staff. Because much of what we do is a group effort, I refer to HG as "us" and "we" (the team as a whole) as opposed to "me" and "I" (an individual). The exception is when I have a personal story to share, because saying the awesome chili recipe was invented by "our husband" would be silly (and illegal in most states!).

Is Hungry Girl a chef?

Sort of, but not by traditional standards. And this is not a typical cookbook. If you're looking for fancy, formal "chef-like" recipes you've definitely come to the wrong place. This book is filled with simple, fun, easy recipes that use lots of packaged foods and shortcuts to make great-tasting guilt-free snacks and meals. If you aspire to be a gourmet chef, there are more appropriate books out there for you. But if you want to prepare awesome, tongue-pleasing foods that won't send you out shopping for bigger pants, you've got the right book!

What makes a recipe "guilt-free"?

When it comes to HG recipes, our goal is to make them delicious—but also to keep them low in fat and calories (that's the guilt-free part!). We also aim for high-fiber counts, because we love fiber (it's good for you, and it fills you up!). Even though we mostly focus on calories and fat, we provide nutritional information for carbs, sugars, protein, etc., so you can tweak any recipe to meet your needs. For example, people concerned about sodium can simply use low-salt versions of canned items called for in our recipes.

Is there a Hungry Girl diet plan?

No, there is no Hungry Girl diet plan. While there are HG recipes for breakfast, lunch, snacks, and more, the idea is to incorporate these recipes into an eating plan that works for you.

Why a Hungry Girl book?

Hungry-Girl.com offers many recipes. They have become the most sought-after content we provide. Over the years, we've received thousands of requests for a Hungry Girl recipe book, and we agreed that it was a good idea. So here ya go!

Why don't you use as many name brands in the book as you do on the site?

As you read this book, you'll see that while some of the recipes call for very specific name-brand items, most do not. The idea behind this is to keep the recipes as generic as possible, so people can easily find all the items they need at local supermarkets. The nutritional information in the book has been carefully calculated based on the averages of *many* brands, so you don't have to find our favorite low-calorie picks for your recipes to have the same stats. When a very specific ingredient is super-important to a recipe (like it simply will *not* taste the same or have as impressive nutritional stats without it), we will call out the name brands and specific products needed. We feature more specific products in our daily emails because we can easily give you up-to-the-minute information on where to purchase them. We simply can't do that in this book. (For a list of our recommended brands, see page 6.)

What happens if I make substitutions for ingredients in some recipes?

Your oven will explode. Okay, not really! You can, of course, make substitutions for products and ingredients, but the taste and nutritional information will vary accordingly, so keep that in mind when swapping.

How was the nutritional information in this book calculated?

The stats for each recipe were carefully calculated using extremely reliable nutritional databases, countless product labels, and by doing extensive research. When recipes call for generic ingredients (like light vanilla soymilk or light bread), we used average nutritional information for those products. Those averages were calculated based on a wide variety of national brands. Also taken into account were the small amounts of calories and fat in many so-called "no-calorie" and "fat-free" ingredients. We take great pride in determining the most accurate nutritional information possible. After all, we make these recipes, too!

Are optional ingredients included in each recipe's nutritional information?

No, they aren't. If you choose to use the optional ingredients listed in the recipes, the nutritional information will change accordingly. However, all optional ingredients are guilt-free items, so they won't add crazy amounts of fat or calories to any of the recipes.

Some of your recipes call for ingredients (like chicken) that are already cooked. What's the best way to cook without adding any fat?

There are so many simple ways to cook chicken, shrimp, and beef without adding fat and calories. Just cook your food in a pan with a spritz of nonstick spray, boil it in a pot of water, or steam it in the microwave or over the stove. Easy!

Typically, HG recipes include Weight Watchers *POINTS*® values. Where can I find Weight Watchers *POINTS*® values for the recipes in this book?

Good question. If you're a Hungry Girl fan, you know how much we love and support Weight Watchers. Their plans are healthy, easy to follow, and can fit into your lifestyle. That's why we co-developed a bunch of recipes with them for this book. For a listing of *POINTS*® values for all the recipes in this book, go to hungry-girl.com/book.

Where can I find photos of all the recipes in this book?

While the book is cute and pretty as is, we know it's important to see photos of our recipes. Luckily, we have pictures of every recipe in this book online at hungry-girl.com/book (and a bunch in the book, too!).

Why are there so many single-serving recipes in this book?

Throughout the years, we've heard over and over how easy Hungry Girl recipes are to make, and how often people prepare food for themselves. Single-serving recipes are ideal for this reason, and HG subscribers always eat up (pun intended) these made-for-one recipes. That being said, it's easy to double, triple, or quadruple any of the single-serving recipes—so you can adjust them to feed as many hungry people as you like. Just don't quadruple a recipe and eat the whole thing yourself, or you'll be in BIG trouble!

How can you have FAQs about the book when this is your first book?

Yep, we've been caught! These aren't really frequently asked questions. They're actually questions we anticipated you might have. But "QWAYMH" didn't sound as good as "FAQs." Now quit asking so many questions and start readin' already!

Hungry Girl's Recommended Products...

We're not shy when it comes to naming names, and it's no secret that we have favorites. While the recipes in the book work well with many different products, we definitely have our favorites as far as taste and nutritional information are concerned. Here are some of our recommendations:

Light Soymilk (Vanilla, Chocolate, or Plain)
8th Continent Light Soymilk
Silk Light Soymilk
Almond Breeze Unsweetened (technically not soymilk, but it's SO good and much lower in calories!)

Fat-Free Liquid Non-Dairy Creamer
Coffee-mate Original Fat Free

Fat-Free Powdered Non-Dairy Creamer
Coffee-mate Original Fat Free

Fat-Free Cheese
Kraft Fat Free Cheese
Lifetime Fat Free Cheese

Reduced-Fat Cheese
Sargento Reduced Fat Deli Style Sliced Cheese
The Laughing Cow Light Cheese Wedges (used in specific recipes)

Light Whipped Butter/Light Buttery Spread
Brummel & Brown
Land O'Lakes Whipped Light Butter
Smart Balance 37% Light Buttery Spread

Fat-Free Liquid Egg Substitute
Better'n Eggs
Egg Beaters Original
Nulaid ReddiEgg

Fat-Free Yogurt
Yoplait Light (for creamier, more decadent yogurt)
Dannon Light & Fit (for extra-low-cal, thinner yogurt)

Fat-Free Greek Yogurt
Fage Total 0%
Oikos Organic

Fat-Free Ice Cream
Breyers Double Churn FREE
Dreyer's/Edy's Slow Churned Light (not completely fat-free, but
    it's awesome and will barely affect recipe nutritional information)

Light Bread and Buns
Weight Watchers Bread
Wonder Light Bread and Buns
Nature's Own Light Bread and Double Fiber Wheat Buns
Arnold Bakery Light Bread
Pepperidge Farm Light Style Bread, Very Thin Bread,
    and Classic Whole Grain Buns
Sara Lee Delightful Bread

Whole Wheat (or High Fiber) Pitas
Weight Watchers 100% Whole Wheat Pita Pocket Bread
Western Bagel The Alternative Pita Bread

Light English Muffins
Weight Watchers English Muffins
Thomas' Light Multi-Grain English Muffins
Thomas' 100 Calorie Original English Muffins
Western Bagel Alternative English Muffins

Low-Fat Flour Tortillas

La Tortilla Factory Whole Wheat Low-Carb/Low-Fat Tortillas (sometimes labeled Smart & Delicious Low Carb High Fiber), large

Mission Carb Balance, Soft Taco Size

Tumaro's 8-inch Low in Carbs or Healthy Flour Tortillas

Boneless Skinless Lean Chicken Breast

Tyson Fresh Boneless, Skinless Chicken Breasts

Perdue Fit & Easy Boneless, Skinless Chicken Breasts

Fat-Free or Nearly Fat-Free Hot Dogs

Hebrew National 97% Fat Free Beef Franks

Hoffy Extra Lean Beef Franks

Yves Meatless Hot Dogs or Tofu Dogs

Ball Park Fat Free Franks or Bun Size Smoked White Turkey Franks

Ground-Beef-Style or Sausage-Style Soy Crumbles

Boca Meatless Burgers (ground-beef style)

Morningstar Farms Meal Starters Grillers Recipe Crumbles (ground-beef style)

Morningstar Farms Meal Starters Sausage Style Recipe Crumbles

Veggie Burger Patties

Gardenburger Veggie Burgers

Morningstar Farms Garden Veggie Patties

Dr. Praeger's Veggie Burgers (blot the oil!)

Amy's Veggie Burgers

Low-Fat Turkey or Veggie Chili

Boca Meatless Chili (found in the freezer aisle)

Health Valley Chili (no-salt-added versions available!)

Dan Good Chili (recipe on page 122)

Extra-Lean Turkey Bacon

Jennie-O Extra Lean Turkey Bacon

Extra Lean Ground Turkey
Jennie-O Extra Lean Ground Turkey Breast
Butterball Extra Lean Ground Turkey Breast

Turkey Pepperoni
Hormel Turkey Pepperoni

Breaded-Chicken-Style Soy Patty
Boca Meatless Chik'n Patties Original
Morningstar Farms Chik Patties Original

Baked Tortilla Chips
Guiltless Gourmet Tortilla Chips
Baked! Tostitos

Rice Cakes/Mini Rice Cakes/Soy Crisps
Quaker Rice Snacks and Soy Crisps

Freeze-Dried Fruit
Gerber Organic Mini Fruits (found in the baby-food aisle)
Crispy Green Crispy Fruit (crispygreen.com)
Just Tomatoes, Etc. (justtomatoes.com)

Sugar-Free Maple Syrup
Cary's Sugar Free Syrup
Mrs. Butterworth's Sugar Free Syrup
Log Cabin Sugar Free Syrup
Joseph's Sugar Free Syrup

No-Calorie Sweetener Packets
Splenda No Calorie Sweetener

Sugar-Free Calorie-Free Syrup
Torani Sugar Free Syrup

Sugar-Free Powdered Drink Mix Packets
Crystal Light On The Go
Wyler's Light Singles to go!
Market Pantry single pouch sugar-free drink mix

Salad Dressing
Wish-Bone Salad Spritzers
Hidden Valley The Original Ranch Fat Free
Wish-Bone Light!
Litehouse Vinaigrettes (check labels for the low-calorie ones)

Nonstick Spray
Pam No-Stick Cooking Spray

Canned Brands We Love
S&W (low-calorie and low-sodium options)
Health Valley (fat-free, low-salt, and no-salt broth options)
Libby's (high-quality pure pumpkin)

Visit hungry-girl.com/book for updated versions of this list.

HG's TOP ATE Kitchen Essentials

This book is packed with simple recipes that anyone can make. The instructions are clear and easy, and you won't find words like "sift," "blanch," or "emulsify." So you don't need any fancy cooking dictionary to help you. What you *do* need is a bunch of things that will help make your HG recipe endeavors easier. They are as follows:

1. Measuring cups. Those little measuring cup sets definitely come in handy. One measuring cup will do, but those cute little sets are better (and they're *cheap*).

2. A basic food scale. Most of the ingredients are measured by cup, but occasionally certain ingredients require you to weigh your food. A simple scale—preferably digital—with weight measurements in both grams and ounces works best.

3. A very good blender. Food processors are okay, but a good blender is exactly what you need to help you with the recipes in this book. (And blenders are super-easy to use and clean.)

4. Nice pots and pans. You don't necessarily need the most expensive or fancy bakeware, but you do need some functional pots and pans in a variety of sizes.

5. An electric mixer. You can easily find cheapie-cheap versions of this kitchen staple at any store that sells home appliances. No need to get one that's too fancy or pricey!

6. Measuring spoons. *Never* use regular serving spoons to measure ingredients for recipes. Sticking with actual measuring spoons is the only way to get accurate measurements and calorie counts.

7. Lots of nonstick cooking spray. Never let your kitchen run out of this stuff. It's used in a huge number of HG recipes. Keep extra cans on hand to be safe.

8. Good ice. Wimpy ice is bad. Old ice is worse. Keep lots of large, fresh ice cubes on hand. Do whatever it takes to make that happen. Please!

Other things you may want to have on hand: cute glasses (for our drinks and cocktails), fun straws, lots of food-storage containers, and a George Foreman Grill (for grilling up all the chicken our recipes call for!).

chapter one

rise & dine

breakfast
wake up. it's time to chew things.

Breakfast may be the most important meal of the day, but it can also be the most challenging. Who has time to think about what to eat in the morning—or the energy to prepare it? Ugh. Here's the deal: Skipping breakfast is a bad idea, and hitting the drive-thru can be an even worse one. The breakfasts in this chapter are very easy to make (really), and they're superdelicious. Try them out, and many of these will become staples in your life.
Rise and dine!

yumtastic breakfast burrito

PER SERVING (1 burrito): 239 calories, 3g fat, 1,111mg sodium, 27g carbs, 9g fiber, 4g sugars, 29g protein

✳ Ingredients

1 medium low-fat flour tortilla (about 110 calories with at least 6g fiber)
2 slices (about 1 ounce) extra-lean turkey bacon
½ cup fat-free liquid egg substitute
1 slice fat-free American cheese

✳ Directions

Cook bacon according to package directions, either in a pan with nonstick spray or in the microwave. Set aside.

Pour egg substitute into a pan spritzed with nonstick spray and scramble over medium heat until fluffy and solid.

Heat tortilla in the microwave until slightly warm. Place cheese in the center of the tortilla. Top with eggs and bacon.

Build your burrito by first folding in the sides and then rolling the tortilla up from the bottom. Heat in the microwave (seam-side down) for an additional 15 to 20 seconds.

MAKES 1 SERVING

super-duper veggie scramble

PER SERVING (entire recipe): 183 calories, 3g fat, 614mg sodium, 17g carbs, 5g fiber, 5g sugars, 22g protein

✳ Ingredients

1 veggie burger patty, thawed if previously frozen
½ cup fat-free liquid egg substitute
¼ cup chopped tomatoes
¼ cup chopped mushrooms
2 tablespoons chopped onions

✳ Directions

Chop veggie patty into bite-sized pieces. Place mushrooms, onions, and veggie patty pieces in a pan spritzed with nonstick spray, and cook over medium heat for 2 minutes.

Add egg substitute and tomatoes to the pan. Scramble together until eggs are cooked.

MAKES 1 SERVING

CHEW ON THIS:

An average bacon, egg, and cheese breakfast sandwich contains about 500 calories and 25 fat grams! You can eat 2 POUNDS of scrambled Egg Beaters and still not reach that calorie (or fat) count.

smokin' salmon cream cheese roll-up

PER SERVING (entire recipe): 239 calories, 5.5g fat, 1,475mg sodium, 28g carbs, 9.5g fiber, 3g sugars, 24g protein

✶ Ingredients

1 medium low-fat flour tortilla (about 110 calories with at least 6g fiber)

2½ ounces smoked salmon

2 tablespoons fat-free cream cheese

2 tablespoons chopped red onions

2 slices tomato, halved

✶ Directions

Heat tortilla in the microwave until slightly warm. Lay tortilla out on a flat surface.

Spread cream cheese evenly on top of tortilla. Place salmon in the middle. Top with tomatoes and onions. Wrap it up by folding in tortilla sides and then roll up from the bottom.

MAKES 1 SERVING

BITE IT!

Cup of Oatmeal—120 calories, 2.5g fat

Side of Fruit—80 calories, <0.5g fat

2 Egg Whites—35 calories, 0g fat

1 Pancake—120 calories, 3g fat

FIGHT IT!

Cup of Granola—400 calories, 10g fat

Side of Hash Browns—200 calories, 15g fat

2 Eggs—150 calories, 10g fat

Slice of French Toast—200 calories, 8g fat

Nutritional information based on averages (not including added toppings like milk, butter, or syrup).

fancy-schmancy oatmeal

PER SERVING (entire recipe): 183 calories, 2.5g fat, 187mg sodium, 35g carbs, 5.5g fiber, 2g sugars, 7g protein

✳ ✳ *I love oatmeal. The problem for me is that one serving of oatmeal isn't enough to fill me up (come on—are they SERIOUS?). Adding pumpkin to it makes it way more filling, and it adds some extra fiber as well. A double whammy! Feel free to use these same ingredients to add a little zazzle to instant oatmeal, too!* ✳ ✳

✳ Ingredients

½ cup regular oats (not instant)
3 tablespoons canned pure pumpkin
1 tablespoon sugar-free maple syrup
¼ teaspoon cinnamon
1 no-calorie sweetener packet
Dash of salt

✳ Directions

Bring 1 cup of water to a boil in a small pot (use less water for thicker oatmeal, and more water for thinner oatmeal).

Add oats and reduce heat to medium. Stirring occasionally, cook for 5 minutes.

Add pumpkin, maple syrup, cinnamon, sweetener, and salt to the pot and stir. Spoon into a bowl and enjoy.

MAKES 1 SERVING

bring on the breakfast pizza

PER SERVING (1 pizza): 127 calories, <0.5g fat, 762mg sodium, 9g carbs, 1.5g fiber, 5g sugars, 22g protein

✷ ✷ This is definitely one of the cutest b-fast recipes ever. The key to making this one pretty is to carefully craft your egg crust. It's really not that complicated. If I can do it, anyone can. ✷ ✷

✷ Ingredients

½ cup fat-free liquid egg substitute
¼ cup shredded fat-free mozzarella cheese
¼ cup canned tomato sauce
2 tablespoons chopped green bell peppers
2 tablespoons chopped mushrooms
Optional: salt, black pepper, oregano, garlic powder, onion powder,
     red pepper flakes, etc.

✷ Directions

Season tomato sauce to taste with optional ingredients, if desired, and set sauce aside.

Bring a small pan sprayed with nonstick spray to low heat. Pour in egg substitute. Cover and then cook for 3 minutes, or until egg "crust" starts to form.

Carefully flip your egg. Cover and cook for another minute. While egg crust is cooking, microwave chopped veggies for 30 seconds.

Next, top your egg crust with tomato sauce, cheese, and then veggies. Cover again and cook over low heat for 2 minutes, or until cheese is melted. If you like, top with optional spices.

MAKES 1 SERVING

 For a pic of this recipe, see the photo insert. Yay!

· ·

Betcha Didn't Know . . .

The average donut contains just 200 calories and 10 grams of fat, while the average muffin has about 450 calories and 15 grams of fat!

cinnamonlicious french toast

PER SERVING (3 slices): 195 calories, 1g fat, 535mg sodium, 32g carbs, 8g fiber, 4g sugars, 19g protein

✳ ✳ *This French toast is super on its own, but feel free to serve it with sugar-free maple syrup, sugar-free preserves, fresh berries, and/or a squirt of fat-free whipped cream. I also like making this French toast into sticks. If you want to try it that way, just cut the bread into strips before dipping it into the egg wash. You'll feel like you're eating more that way, too!* ✳ ✳

✳ Ingredients

3 slices light bread (40 to 45 calories each with about 2g fiber per slice)

½ cup fat-free liquid egg substitute

½ teaspoon cinnamon, divided

¼ teaspoon vanilla extract

1 no-calorie sweetener packet

✳ Directions

Combine egg substitute with vanilla extract and half of the cinnamon (¼ teaspoon). Use the egg mixture as an egg wash, and dip your bread into it.

Cook bread over medium heat in a pan sprayed with nonstick spray, flipping after a few minutes. Once both sides are brown, plate 'em, and sprinkle with sweetener and the remaining ¼ teaspoon of cinnamon.

MAKES 1 SERVING

For Weight Watchers **POINTS**® values and photos of all the recipes in this book, check out hungry-girl.com/book.

eggamuffin 101

PER SERVING (entire recipe): 184 calories, 2g fat, 870mg sodium, 26g carbs, 6g fiber, 3g sugars, 20g protein

✶ Ingredients

1 light English muffin
1 slice extra-lean ham
1 slice fat-free American cheese
¼ cup fat-free liquid egg substitute

✶ Directions

Toast English muffin to your preference.

Cook egg substitute over medium-high heat in a pan sprayed with nonstick spray.

Place cheese on the bottom half of the muffin, followed by the egg, ham, and then the muffin top.

MAKES 1 SERVING

Would You Rather . . .

If you order a deluxe breakfast sandwich at the drive-thru on the way to work, it'll cost you about 550 calories and as much as 40 grams of fat! To burn that off, you would have to:

✶ Stand and file papers for 3½ hours *or*

✶ Hover over the computer keyboard typing vigorously for more than 5½ hours *or*

✶ Sit in traffic for almost 6 hours! (Whoa . . . what a waste of gas!)

Times based on estimates for a 150-pound woman.

tutti frutti crunch yogurt parfait

PER SERVING (1 parfait): 210 calories, 1g fat, 147mg sodium, 45g carbs, 3.5g fiber, 31g sugars, 10g protein

✳ Ingredients

6 ounces fat-free vanilla yogurt
6 apple cinnamon soy crisps or mini rice cakes, crushed
½ cup sliced strawberries
½ cup blueberries

✳ Directions

Place one-third of the strawberries and blueberries in the bottom of a tall glass. Add half of the yogurt.

Top with another third of the blueberries and strawberries. Cover with half of the apple cinnamon crunchies.

Spoon the remaining yogurt on top and cover with remaining fruit and crunchies.

MAKES 1 SERVING

 For a pic of this recipe, see the photo insert. Yay!

blueberry apple pancake shake-up

PER SERVING (3 pancakes): 252 calories, 2.5g fat, 517mg sodium, 44g carbs, 4g fiber, 12g sugars, 13g protein

✳ Ingredients

⅓ cup regular oats (not instant)
2 tablespoons dry pancake mix
⅓ cup peeled and finely chopped apples
¼ cup blueberries
¼ cup fat-free liquid egg substitute
1 tablespoon fat-free cottage cheese
¼ teaspoon vanilla extract
1 tablespoon Splenda No Calorie
    Sweetener (granulated)
Dash of salt

✳ Directions

Place all ingredients except for the blueberries and apples in a medium bowl. Add 3 tablespoons of water and stir until thoroughly mixed.

Gently fold in apples and blueberries.

Over medium heat, in a large pan sprayed with nonstick spray, evenly pour batter to form 3 pancakes. Once pancakes begin to look solid (after about 3 minutes), gently flip.

Cook for 3 additional minutes, or until both sides are lightly browned and insides are cooked through. Now plate your pancakes and enjoy.

MAKES 1 SERVING

blueberry mango madness smoothie

PER SERVING (entire recipe): 165 calories, 1g fat, 10mg sodium, 42g carbs, 6g fiber, 31g sugars, 1g protein

✳ Ingredients

1 cup frozen blueberries, slightly thawed
¾ cup frozen mango chunks, slightly thawed
½ packet (one 5-calorie serving) sugar-free powdered orange drink mix

✳ Directions

Combine drink mix with 8 ounces of cold water. Stir well.

Place fruit and drink mixture into a blender, and puree until thoroughly mixed. If blending slows, stop blender, stir mixture, and blend again. Pour into a tall glass and enjoy!

MAKES 1 SERVING

For Weight Watchers *POINTS*® values and photos of all the recipes in this book, check out hungry-girl.com/book.

ginormous cereal bowl-anza

PER SERVING (1 bowl): 286 calories, 3g fat, 253mg sodium, 60g carbs, 10g fiber, 12g sugars, 12g protein

✶ ✶ Cereal is typically one of my "danger foods" because the recommended serving sizes are laughable, so I end up eating WAY too much of the stuff. And huge bowls of cereal = too many calories. This recipe allows you to eat a seriously gigantic bowl for a reasonable amount of calories. I LOVE, LOVE this breakfast! ✶ ✶

✶ Ingredients

1 cup light vanilla soymilk
1 cup puffed wheat cereal
1 cup puffed rice cereal
½ cup puffed corn cereal (like Kix)
¼ cup Fiber One bran cereal (original)
¼ cup blueberries

✶ Directions

Place all ingredients in a bowl and cover with soymilk. Tada!

MAKES 1 SERVING

HG Heads Up!
The average cereal serving size is a cup or less. The average cereal bowl holds *way* more than that. Fill up that bowl, and there's a good chance you'll be sucking down two to three servings—and two to three times the fat and calories.

eggs bene-chick

PER SERVING (entire recipe): 183 calories, 8g fat, 627mg sodium, 16g carbs, 3g fiber, 3g sugars, 13g protein

✶✶ *For years I avoided Eggs Benedict because it's LOADED with fat and calories. This recipe was created out of sheer necessity (or should I say desperation?).* ✶✶

✶ Ingredients

½ light English muffin
1 large egg
1 slice extra-lean ham
1 tablespoon fat-free mayonnaise
1 teaspoon Hellmann's/Best Foods Dijonnaise
1 teaspoon light whipped butter or light buttery spread, softened
1 teaspoon lemon yogurt (or plain yogurt with a squirt of lemon juice)

✶ Directions

To make sauce, combine mayo, Dijonnaise, butter, and yogurt. Set aside.

Crack egg gently into a small cup or dish, and set that aside as well.

Fill a medium pot with 2 inches of water, and bring water to a boil. Once boiling, lower temperature until a steady and consistent (but *very* low) boil is reached.

Gently pour the egg into the pot, and allow it to cook for 3 to 5 minutes (3 for a runnier egg, 5 for a very firm one), or until egg white is mostly opaque. Carefully remove egg by sliding a spatula underneath it and placing it on a plate. Use a paper towel to soak up any excess water.

Heat ham and muffin (toast muffin, if desired).

Heat sauce in the microwave for about 20 seconds and give it a stir (add more water if you prefer a thinner sauce). Top muffin with ham and egg, then cover with sauce.

MAKES 1 SERVING

 For a pic of this recipe, see the photo insert. Yay!

• •

Breakfast Shockers!
Steer clear of these b-fast blunders . . .

❋ **Denny's Fabulous French Toast Platter** (1,261 calories, 79g fat)
Nothing fabulous about this French flub!

❋ **Burger King DOUBLE CROISSAN'WICH w/Double Sausage** (680 calories, 51g fat)
Croissant + Sausage = Calorie Catastrophe

❋ **McDonald's Deluxe Breakfast w/syrup and margarine** (1,330 calories, 64g fat)
1,330 calories for breakfast? How embarrassing!

❋ **Hardee's Loaded Breakfast Burrito** (780 calories, 51g fat)
It's loaded alright—with FAT!

chapter two

chop 'til ya drop

chopped salads
hack your salads. all the cool kids are doing it.

Why is there a whole chapter devoted to *chopped* salads, you ask? Because chopped salads are so much more fun and exciting than regular salads. They're *way* easier to eat, too (there are no unwieldy lettuce pieces to awkwardly shove in your mouth). That being said, if you're too lazy to hack your ingredients, or just not into chopped salads for some reason, feel free to make any of the salads in this chapter without chopping 'em up. They'll still taste great. As for dressing, the majority of the salads here are listed without it. Use your dressing of choice with any of the recipes, but please be sure to read labels carefully, because even low-fat and fat-free dressings can contain lots of calories. And remember, any time a recipe calls for an ingredient cooked in advance, use nonstick spray or nothing at all. Happy chopping!

rockin' & choppin' taco salad

PER SERVING (1 salad): 286 calories, 3.5g fat, 920mg sodium, 42g carbs, 12g fiber, 7g sugars, 24g protein

✳✳ *The big difference between this taco salad and so many high-calorie alternatives is that this one lacks that ridiculously fatty tortilla shell. Good riddance to that! By the way, this salad tastes great with salsa!* ✳✳

✳ Ingredients

3 cups chopped romaine lettuce
⅔ cup low-fat veggie chili
¼ cup chopped tomatoes
¼ cup shredded fat-free cheddar cheese
2 tablespoons fat-free sour cream
1 tablespoon chopped or sliced black olives
6 baked tortilla chips, crushed
¼ teaspoon taco seasoning mix, dry

✳ Directions

Prepare chili as directed on package. Set aside.

Place lettuce in a large bowl. Top with tomatoes. Add chili and cheese.

Top with olives and sour cream. Then finish off by adding crushed tortilla chips and sprinkling taco seasoning on top.

MAKES 1 SERVING

buffalo chicken choppity chop

PER SERVING (1 salad): 192 calories, 3g fat, 848mg sodium, 15g carbs, 5g fiber, 5g sugars, 29g protein

✱✱ *To make this salad taste* exactly *like buffalo wings, you need to use original Frank's RedHot. If you substitute another hot sauce, you may not get the same result. Just a friendly little warning . . .*✱✱

✶ Ingredients

3 cups chopped romaine lettuce

3 ounces cooked boneless skinless lean chicken breast, chopped

1 tablespoon Frank's RedHot Original Cayenne Pepper Sauce

1 tablespoon reduced-fat Parmesan-style grated topping

½ cup chopped carrots

¼ cup chopped celery

✶ Directions

Place chicken in a small microwave-safe dish. Top with hot sauce and Parmesan. Stir until chicken is coated, then heat for 45 seconds in the microwave.

Place lettuce, carrots, and celery in a large bowl, and then top with the chicken mixture.

MAKES 1 SERVING

For Weight Watchers *POINTS*®
values and photos of all the
recipes in this book, check out
hungry-girl.com/book.

crazy-delicious cobby chop

PER SERVING (1 salad): 223 calories, 3g fat, 565mg sodium, 16g carbs, 6.5g fiber, 8g sugars, 36g protein

✶ Ingredients

3 cups chopped romaine lettuce

2 ounces cooked boneless skinless lean chicken breast, chopped

2 slices (about 1 ounce) extra-lean turkey bacon

½ cup cooked and chopped asparagus

½ cup chopped tomatoes

¼ cup canned beets, drained and chopped

1 large hard-boiled egg white, chopped

2 tablespoons shredded fat-free mozzarella cheese

1 teaspoon minced scallions

✶ Directions

Cook bacon according to package directions, either in a pan with nonstick spray or in the microwave. Once cool enough to handle, chop and set aside.

Place lettuce in a large bowl.

Add your chopped ingredients by placing them on top of the lettuce in individual rows in this order: turkey bacon, cheese, asparagus, chicken, tomatoes, egg white, and beets.

Sprinkle the scallions on top and enjoy!

MAKES 1 SERVING

retro-rific chopped chef salad

PER SERVING (1 salad): 220 calories, 5.5g fat, 943mg sodium, 15g carbs, 4g fiber, 7g sugars, 29g protein

✶ ✶ *I remember eating chef salad as a child, thinking it was the world's healthiest lunch. Boy was I wrong. But this version is completely guilt-free and delicious. And the calories are so low you can splurge with a little Thousand Island dressing, but stick with the low-fat kind!* ✶ ✶

✶ Ingredients

3 cups chopped romaine lettuce

1 ounce cooked skinless lean turkey breast, chopped

1 ounce cooked roast beef, chopped

1 ounce cooked ham, chopped

1 Roma tomato, chopped

½ medium cucumber, chopped

1 slice fat-free American cheese, chopped

✶ Directions

Throw all the ingredients in a large bowl, toss, and then serve. Yum.

MAKES 1 SERVING

Salads: Friend or Foe?

See how your favorites stack up . . .

Chinese Chicken Salad—885 calories, 50g fat

Taco Salad w/Tortilla Shell—810 calories, 48g fat

Chef Salad—500 calories, 35g fat

Chicken Caesar Salad—775 calories, 56g fat

Cobb Salad—615 calories, 41g fat

Nutritional information based on averages (dressing included).

hacked 'n whacked
santa fe shrimp supreme

PER SERVING (1 salad with dressing): 380 calories, 4g fat,
825mg sodium, 62g carbs, 11.5g fiber, 16g sugars, 28g protein

✳ Ingredients

For Salad

3 cups chopped romaine lettuce

3 ounces cooked shrimp

1 small corn tortilla

½ cup grape tomatoes, halved

½ cup chopped red onions

½ cup chopped bell peppers (any color)

¼ cup canned black beans, rinsed and drained

¼ cup canned sweet corn kernels, drained

1 tablespoon white wine vinegar

1 tablespoon lime juice

1 no-calorie sweetener packet

¼ teaspoon taco seasoning mix, dry

Optional: 1 tablespoon chopped cilantro

For Dressing

3 tablespoons fat-free ranch dressing

1½ teaspoons tomato paste

¼ teaspoon taco seasoning mix, dry

✳ Directions

Preheat oven to 400 degrees.

Cut tortilla into matchstick-sized strips. Lightly spray a small baking pan with nonstick spray, and place strips in the center of the pan.

Sprinkle ¼ teaspoon of taco seasoning over tortilla strips, and carefully toss them to evenly distribute seasoning. Spread strips out on the pan, place in the oven, and cook for 5 to 7 minutes, until strips look crispy. Remove strips, and set aside.

In a small dish, combine 2 tablespoons of water with vinegar, lime juice, and sweetener, as well as cilantro, if using. Place peppers and onions in a small microwave-safe dish, and pour vinegar mixture over veggies. Cover and heat in the microwave for 2 minutes.

Add black beans and corn to the veggies. Stir well and then drain vinegar mixture. Place dish in the fridge until chilled.

Once ready to serve, place lettuce in a large bowl and top with veggie/bean mixture. Add shrimp, tomatoes, and tortilla strips.

Mix dressing ingredients together in a small dish and serve alongside salad.

MAKES 1 SERVING

 For a pic of this recipe, see the photo insert. Yay!

· ·

TOP ATE Salad Disasters
In no particular order . . .

1. Fried Noodles (100 calories and 5g fat!)
2. Croutons (75 calories and 3g fat!)
3. Bacon (90 calories and 7g fat!)
4. Oil-Soaked Veggies (100 calories and 10g fat!)
5. Mayo-Laden Items (150 calories and 10g fat!)
6. Creamy Dressings (150 calories and 15g fat!)
7. Full-Fat Cheeses (100 calories and 8g fat!)
8. Tortilla Shells (300 calories and 20g fat!)

Nutritional information based on averages for a typical serving.

sliced 'n diced fajita steak salad

PER SERVING (1 salad): 253 calories, 5g fat, 540mg sodium, 30g carbs, 6.5g fiber, 8g sugars, 25g protein

✳ Ingredients

3 cups chopped romaine lettuce

3 ounces raw boneless lean top sirloin steak, sliced

4 ounces Diet Coke

½ small onion, sliced

½ medium yellow bell pepper, sliced

½ medium red bell pepper, sliced

4 baked tortilla chips, crushed

¼ cup salsa

2 tablespoons fat-free sour cream

✳ Directions

Soak steak strips in Diet Coke (use a small bowl). Refrigerate for 30 minutes.

Spray a pan with nonstick spray and set heat to medium-high. Once pan is hot, add steak strips and all of the cola marinade to the pan.

Cook for 1 to 2 minutes, or until outside surface of steak is no longer pink (do not overcook). Remove meat, leaving excess marinade in the pan, and set aside.

Turn heat down to medium. Add onion to the pan with the remaining marinade. Cook onion for about 2 minutes and then add the peppers.

Cook for 1 minute, return steak strips to the pan, and cook for 1 additional minute.

Place lettuce in a large bowl and top with the steak/veggie mixture. Finish off by adding crushed chips, salsa, and sour cream.

MAKES 1 SERVING

Dressing Undressed . . .
The naked truth behind some of your favorite salad dressings . . .

Caesar—160 calories, 17g fat
Blue Cheese—160 calories, 16g fat
Ranch—150 calories, 16g
Italian—100 calories, 8g fat
Thousand Island—120 calories, 11g fat
Vinaigrette—130 calories, 13g fat
French—150 calories, 14g fat

Nutritional information based on averages for a 2-tablespoon serving.

chinese chicken chop

PER SERVING (1 salad): 245 calories, 2g fat, 129mg sodium, 35g carbs, 10g fiber, 16g sugars, 29g protein

✳ Ingredients

2 cups chopped romaine lettuce

1 cup shredded green cabbage

3 ounces cooked boneless skinless lean chicken breast, chopped

½ cup canned mandarin oranges in juice, drained

½ cup canned sliced water chestnuts,
     drained and chopped

2 tablespoons minced scallions

2 tablespoons Fiber One bran cereal (original)

✳ Directions

Place lettuce and cabbage in a large bowl and toss.

Add oranges and water chestnuts, and then top with chicken.

Sprinkle scallions and Fiber One over salad.

MAKES 1 SERVING

the hg special

PER SERVING (1 salad): 308 calories, 5.5g fat, 525mg sodium, 36g carbs, 9g fiber, 11g sugars, 34g protein

✶✶ *I love this salad sooooo much. It's been a staple in my life for years. I'm happy to finally share it with the world. P.S. Do not fear beets. They work really well here.* ✶✶

✶ Ingredients

3 cups chopped romaine lettuce

3 ounces cooked boneless skinless lean chicken breast, chopped

1 Roma tomato, chopped

½ medium cucumber, chopped

¼ cup shredded carrots

¼ cup canned beets, drained and chopped

2 tablespoons canned sweet corn kernels

2 tablespoons chopped red onions

2 tablespoons canned garbanzo beans (chickpeas)

2 tablespoons reduced-fat Parmesan-style grated topping

✶ Directions

Place all ingredients in a bowl and toss well to mix.

MAKES 1 SERVING

hot chick bbq chop

PER SERVING (1 salad): 320 calories, 2.5g fat, 929mg sodium, 48g carbs, 10g fiber, 26g sugars, 32g protein

✳ Ingredients

For Salad

3 cups chopped romaine lettuce

3 ounces cooked boneless skinless lean chicken breast, chopped

½ medium cucumber, chopped

½ cup chopped tomatoes

⅓ cup chopped jicama

¼ cup chopped red onions

2 tablespoons canned sweet corn kernels

2 tablespoons canned black beans

Optional: 1 tablespoon chopped cilantro

For Sauce

¼ cup canned tomato sauce

2 tablespoons ketchup

2 teaspoons brown sugar (not packed)

2 teaspoons cider vinegar

½ teaspoon garlic powder

✳ Directions

Combine all sauce ingredients in a small bowl. Coat chicken in sauce. Heat, if desired.

Place all other ingredients in a bowl and toss until mixed.

Top salad with BBQ chicken and enjoy!

MAKES 1 SERVING

. . . .

The Greens Scene

Get salad savvy in just seconds . . .

✳ **When buying dressing at the market, *always* read labels very carefully. Even those labeled "light" or "reduced-fat" can contain tons of fat and calories.**

✳ **At a restaurant? Play it safe and go with a drizzle of olive oil (for those healthy fats) and some vinegar or a squirt of lemon. You can also carry low-cal dressing packets in your purse, or request some of the awesome alternatives listed here!**

✳ **There are many alternatives to fatty dressings that will save calories and fat, but still pack a flavorful punch! Do your waist a favor and reach for salsa, soy sauce, balsamic or red wine vinegar, lemon juice, or Dijon mustard!**

✳ **Always dip—never pour dressing directly on your salad. You'll use way less and save calories and fat.**

chop-tastic veggie salad

PER SERVING (1 salad): 206 calories, 3.5g fat, 405mg sodium, 33g carbs, 11g fiber, 13g sugars, 14g protein

✳ Ingredients

3 cups chopped romaine lettuce
1 veggie burger patty (veggie-based rather than the imitation-meat kind)
½ cup chopped red and/or yellow bell peppers
½ cup chopped zucchini and/or yellow squash
½ cup chopped tomatoes
½ cup chopped red onions

✳ Directions

Prepare veggie patty according to the package directions (preferably grilled in a pan with nonstick spray so the outside is crispy).

Place lettuce in a bowl and layer all the veggies on top of it.

Chop veggie patty into bite-sized pieces and evenly distribute on top of salad.

MAKES 1 SERVING

For Weight Watchers *POINTS*® values and photos of all the recipes in this book, check out hungry-girl.com/book.

hacked 'n whacked blt salad

This recipe was co-developed with Weight Watchers®.

✴✴ *This one tastes EXACTLY like a BLT!* ✴✴

✴ Ingredients

3 cups chopped romaine lettuce

6 slices (about 3 ounces) extra-lean turkey bacon

2 Roma tomatoes, chopped

1 slice light bread (40 to 45 calories with about 2g fiber)

✴ Directions

Toast the bread slice and set it aside to cool and harden.

Cook bacon according to package directions, either in a pan with nonstick spray or in the microwave. Once cool enough to handle, chop and set aside.

Put lettuce and tomatoes in a large bowl. Top with bacon pieces.

Cut bread into bite-sized pieces and put on top of the salad.

MAKES 1 SERVING

pizzalicious chop chop

PER SERVING (1 salad): 206 calories, 6g fat, 770mg sodium, 19g carbs, 6g fiber, 8g sugars, 19g protein

✳ Ingredients

3 cups chopped romaine lettuce

10 bite-sized pieces (about ⅔ ounce) turkey pepperoni, chopped

1 large Roma tomato, chopped

¼ cup chopped green bell peppers

2 tablespoons chopped onions

2 tablespoons sliced black olives

¼ cup shredded fat-free mozzarella cheese

2 teaspoons reduced-fat Parmesan-style grated topping

✳ Directions

In a large bowl combine all salad ingredients. Enjoy!

MAKES 1 SERVING

> **HG Tip:** For extra pizza fun, stir together a dressing of tomato sauce, fat-free broth, and Italian spices. Mmmm!!!

big chomp cheeseburger chop

✶✶ *This salad is the perfect fix for a cheeseburger craving. Whip up a low-cal special-sauce dressing by mixing equal parts fat-free mayo, ketchup, and Dijonnaise. YUM!* ✶✶

✶ Ingredients

3 cups chopped romaine lettuce

1 Boca Meatless Burger, Original

1 slice fat-free cheese (American or cheddar)

4 slices/chips dill pickle

⅓ cup chopped tomatoes

3 tablespoons chopped onions

✶ Directions

Prepare Boca patty according to package directions, in a pan with nonstick spray or in the microwave.

Top patty with cheese slice. Microwave for 20 seconds or until cheese melts. Set aside.

Place lettuce in a large bowl and top with pickles, tomatoes, and onions.

Chop cheese-topped patty into bite-sized pieces and then add to salad.

MAKES 1 SERVING

HG Tip: Swap the pickle chips for cucumber slices and save 310mg sodium.

chapter three

souper douper

soups

grab a spoon. and no slurping, please . . .

Soup is *awesome*. It tastes great, fills you up, and is easy to make. What more could you ask for? Oh, it also helps you cut calories. Studies show that people who eat broth-based soups regularly end up taking in fewer calories throughout the day (it's true!). These soup recipes are all easy to make, really delicious, and low in calories. Keep some in the fridge—they're *great* to have around for a snack or meal-starter. HG Tip: If you're a sodium-counter, you may want to use low-sodium versions of broths and canned items when making these soups.

freakishly good french onion soup

PER SERVING (1 bowl): 113 calories, 4.5g fat, 897mg sodium, 9g carbs, 1.5g fiber, 2g sugars, 10g protein

✷ Ingredients

1 cup fat-free beef broth
¼ cup thinly sliced onions
½ slice light bread (40 to 45 calories each
    with about 2g fiber per slice)
1 slice reduced-fat provolone cheese

✷ Directions

Toast bread and set aside. Combine onions and broth in a small saucepan and cook over low heat for 10 minutes.

Pour soup into a microwave-safe soup bowl. Place toasted bread on top of soup and then cover with cheese. Place bowl in the microwave and heat for about 30 seconds or until cheese melts and begins to bubble.

MAKES 1 SERVING

For Weight Watchers **POINTS**®
values and photos of all the
recipes in this book, check out
hungry-girl.com/book.

perfect plum tomato cabbage soup

PER SERVING (1 generous cup): 35 calories, <0.5g fat, 410mg sodium, 8g carbs, 1.5g fiber, 5g sugars, 1g protein

✴✴ *I am obsessed with this soup! The best way to enjoy it is with Splenda and Frank's RedHot.* ✴✴

✴ Ingredients

4 cups fat-free vegetable broth
6 plum tomatoes, chopped
2 cups chopped green cabbage
Optional: salt, black pepper, garlic salt, Splenda No Calorie Sweetener, Frank's RedHot Original Cayenne Pepper Sauce, Tabasco Pepper Sauce

✴ Directions

Place chopped tomatoes (along with any juice and seeds) in a large pot sprayed with nonstick spray. Cook over medium heat for 2 to 3 minutes, stirring occasionally.

Add broth and cabbage and raise heat to high. Once soup reaches a boil, reduce heat to low and cover. Allow soup to simmer for 5 minutes.

Season to taste with salt, black pepper, and/or any of the other optional ingredients, if desired.

MAKES 5 SERVINGS

egg flower power soup

PER SERVING (1 generous cup): 50 calories, <0.5g fat, 734mg sodium, 6g carbs, 1g fiber, 3g sugars, 6g protein

✳ Ingredients

4 cups fat-free broth (vegetable, chicken, or beef)
½ cup egg whites (about 4 egg whites)
1 small carrot
1 small zucchini
½ medium red bell pepper
3 medium scallions, chopped
1 tablespoon light or low-sodium soy sauce
1 teaspoon lemon juice
Optional: salt, black pepper, 4 lemon wedges

✳ Directions

Pour egg whites into a container with a spout (like a measuring cup). Stir briefly to eliminate any lumps and then set aside.

Cut all veggies into matchstick-sized strips (use a vegetable shredder if you have one). Combine broth, carrots, zucchini, peppers, soy sauce, and lemon juice in a medium pot. Bring to a boil.

Once soup has reached a boil, reduce to medium heat (a low boil) and add scallions. Cook for about 5 minutes, until veggies are limp.

Next, reduce heat to the lowest setting. *Very* slowly pour in egg whites while *very* quickly stirring in one direction. Remove soup from heat immediately. The result will be gorgeous bursts of egg bits in your soup!

If you like, season to taste with salt and black pepper, then serve with lemon wedges.

MAKES 4 SERVINGS

Soup It Up!

These add-ins are the perfect way to turn ordinary broth into a full-on meal!

½ cup fresh or frozen vegetables (50 calories, <0.5g fat)

1 chopped veggie burger patty (100 calories, 2.5g fat)

3 ounces lean chicken, beef, or seafood (100 calories, 2g fat)

½ cup beans—black, kidney, lima, etc. (100 calories, 1g fat)

3 ounces tofu (65 calories, 3g fat)

2 ounces Tofu Shirataki noodles (20 calories, 0.5g fat)

Nutritional information based on averages.

sassy salsa pumpkin soup

PER SERVING (1 generous cup): 177 calories, 1g fat, 991mg sodium, 35g carbs, 8.5g fiber, 8g sugars, 9g protein

✶✶ This recipe was inspired by a Hungry Girl subscriber named Jacqueline. IT ROCKS!!!!! ✶✶

✶ Ingredients

4 cups fat-free broth (chicken or vegetable)

One 15-ounce can pure pumpkin

One 15-ounce can black beans, drained and rinsed

1 cup canned sweet corn kernels

¾ cup salsa

1 tablespoon minced garlic

1 teaspoon chili powder

½ teaspoon ground cumin

Optional toppings: shredded fat-free or low-fat cheese, fat-free sour cream, chopped scallions

✶ Directions

Spray a medium pot with nonstick spray and bring to medium heat on the stove. Place garlic in the pot. Stir and cook for 1 minute. Add broth and spices, and bring to a simmer.

Add pumpkin and mix well. Add the remaining ingredients, stir, and bring soup to a boil. Reduce heat to low and simmer for 10 minutes.

If you like, top each cup with any of the optional ingredients before serving.

MAKES 4 SERVINGS

spicy tomato soup

PER SERVING (1 cup): 76 calories, <0.5g fat, 550mg sodium, 16g carbs, 3.5g fiber, 10g sugars, 3g protein

✴ Ingredients

4 cups chopped plum tomatoes
2 cups V8 100% Vegetable Juice
4 teaspoons fat-free powdered non-dairy creamer
2 teaspoons onion powder
2 teaspoons garlic powder
2 tablespoons Frank's RedHot Original Cayenne Pepper Sauce
Salt and black pepper, to taste

✴ Directions

Cook tomatoes in a large pot over medium heat for 5 minutes or until very soft, stirring occasionally. Remove tomatoes from heat and allow to cool for a few minutes.

Transfer tomatoes to a food processor or blender. Pulse briefly to a pulpy puree. Return tomatoes to the pot and add all additional ingredients.

Stir well and continuously while bringing soup to a near boil. Allow to cool slightly before serving.

MAKES 4 SERVINGS

v10 soup

PER SERVING (1 generous cup): 60 calories, <0.5g fat, 377mg sodium, 14g carbs, 3.5g fiber, 7g sugars, 3g protein

✳✳ *Warning: This soup is jam-packed with an INSANE amount of veggies!!!* ✳✳

✳ Ingredients

4 cups fat-free vegetable broth
2 cups chopped green cabbage
1¼ cups chopped celery
1 cup chopped mushrooms
1 cup bean sprouts
⅔ cup frozen green beans
1 medium zucchini, diced
2 plum tomatoes, diced
¾ cup sliced carrots
½ cup diced onions
5 asparagus spears, chopped
1½ tablespoons tomato paste
1 teaspoon minced garlic
½ teaspoon basil
¼ teaspoon oregano
¼ teaspoon parsley
Salt and black pepper, to taste

✳ Directions

Spray a large pot with nonstick spray. Cook tomatoes, carrots, onions, asparagus, and garlic over low heat for about 5 minutes.

Raise heat to high, add all other ingredients, and stir. Once soup reaches a full boil, lower the heat until soup is just simmering.

Cover and cook for 20 minutes, or until the beans and celery are tender.

MAKES 6 SERVINGS

. . . .

At-a-Glance Soup Glossary

Know what you're getting yourself into . . .

Bisque: A thick cream soup—can be a dieter's nightmare.

Bouillon: This is just a fancy French word for broth. Broth-based soups are your best bet.

Chowder: Rich (not in a good way) and packed with items like potatoes, cheese, and heavy cream. Chowder is filling, but usually fattening. There *are* light options that are so good you'd swear they're the real deal!

Consommé: A clear soup made by boiling meat, vegetables, etc., to extract their nutritive properties and flavor. A thicker version of a broth, consommé is often relatively low in fat and calories.

Cream Of: Soups with a fatty cream-based liquid as the main ingredient. Beware! Look for low-fat versions to get your creamy fix.

Miso: Japanese soup/soup base that's low in calories and high in taste.

noodled-up chicken soup

PER SERVING (1 generous cup): 98 calories, 1g fat, 369mg sodium, 6g carbs, 2g fiber, 2g sugars, 16g protein

✶✶ *This soup is as good as Grandma's chicken noodle soup— and it has a tiny fraction of the calories!* ✶✶

✶ Ingredients

4 cups fat-free chicken broth

12 ounces raw skinless boneless lean chicken breast

2 packages House Foods Tofu Shirataki, Fettuccine Shape

1 cup diced celery

⅔ cup diced mushrooms

⅔ cup diced carrots

¼ cup diced onions

2 teaspoons parsley, divided

2 teaspoons minced garlic

1 teaspoon garlic powder

Salt and black pepper, to taste

Never worked with Tofu Shirataki before? Turn to page 261 for helpful hints!

✶ Directions

Fill a large pot with 8 cups of water. Add chicken breast, garlic powder, and half of the parsley. Set stove to medium-high heat and cook for 20 minutes.

While the chicken is cooking, rinse and drain the shirataki noodles, and pat until thoroughly dry. Cut the noodles into bite-sized pieces and set aside.

Once chicken is fully cooked, pour the contents of the pot into a colander so only the chicken remains. Using two forks shred the chicken into small pieces.

Place all remaining ingredients in the pot, along with the noodles and chicken, and stir well. Bring the soup to a boil and then reduce heat to a simmer. Cover and cook for 15 to 20 minutes.

Turn off the heat and allow the soup to sit for at least 5 minutes.

MAKES 6 SERVINGS

· ·

CHEW ON THIS:

The first soup dates back to 6000 B.C., with the main ingredient being hippopotamus bones. Eeeewwww!

kickin' chicken tortilla soup

PER SERVING (1 generous cup): 101 calories, 1g fat,
650mg sodium, 13g carbs, 1.5g fiber, 4g sugars, 11g protein

✳ ✳ *Heads Up! This one is super-spicy!* ✳ ✳

✳ Ingredients

3 cups fat-free chicken broth
4 ounces cooked lean skinless boneless chicken breast, shredded
1 cup canned diced tomatoes, undrained
½ cup canned sweet corn kernels
½ cup chopped onions
1 tablespoon chopped jalapeño peppers
1 tablespoon lime juice
1 tablespoon fajita seasoning mix
1 teaspoon minced garlic
¼ teaspoon ground cumin
¼ teaspoon chili powder
6 baked tortilla chips, crushed
Optional toppings: cilantro, fat-free sour
    cream, fat-free or low-fat shredded cheese

✳ Directions

In a medium pot sprayed with nonstick spray, cook onions, garlic, seasoning, and spices over medium heat until onions soften, 3 to 5 minutes.

Add chicken broth and bring to a boil. Then reduce heat to low and simmer for 10 minutes.

Add the corn and diced tomatoes, and continue to cook for 5 minutes.

Add chicken, jalapeño, and lime juice. Stir for 2 to 3 minutes to thoroughly blend flavors.

Once ready to serve, top each serving with crushed chips and, if desired, cilantro, sour cream and/or cheese.

MAKES 4 SERVINGS

. . . .

TOP ATE Horrifyingly Fatty Soups
FYI, these stats are for a small 1-cup serving . . .

1. New England Clam Chowder (200 calories and 10g fat!)

2. French Onion Soup w/Cheese & Toasted Bread Topping (220 calories and 10g fat!)

3. Broccoli Cheddar Soup (250 calories and 16g fat!)

4. Cream of Potato Soup (190 calories and 9g fat!)

5. Chicken Tortilla Soup (160 calories and 10g fat!)

6. Corn Chowder (260 calories and 14g fat!)

7. Cream of Tomato Soup (160 calories and 10g fat!)

8. Lobster Bisque (350 calories and 30g fat!!!)

Nutritional information based on averages for 1-cup servings.

rockin' roasted shrimp & asparagus corn chowder

PER SERVING (1½ cups): 182 calories, 1.5g fat, 520mg sodium, 25g carbs, 3.5g fiber, 10g sugars, 18g protein

✷✷ *This could possibly be one of the best-tasting soups of all time!* ✷✷

✷ Ingredients

4 cups fat-free broth (chicken or vegetable)
12 ounces raw peeled and deveined shrimp, tails removed
20 large asparagus spears
2 medium red bell peppers, seeded and chopped
1 medium russet potato, cut into ½-inch cubes
1 cup canned sweet corn kernels
1 cup evaporated fat-free milk
¾ cup chopped scallions
1 teaspoon minced garlic
½ teaspoon thyme
¼ teaspoon cayenne pepper
Salt and black pepper, to taste

✷ Directions

Preheat oven to 425 degrees.

Take asparagus spears in both hands and snap in half. Discard the tough ends. Place asparagus spears and raw shrimp on a baking pan sprayed with nonstick spray.

Spritz shrimp and asparagus with a light mist of nonstick spray and place pan in the oven for about 6 minutes, until shrimp are opaque and cooked through.

Remove shrimp from the pan and set aside. Flip asparagus over and cook for an additional 6 minutes.

Remove asparagus from the oven and cut asparagus and shrimp into bite-sized pieces.

In a large pot sprayed with nonstick spray, cook bell peppers, scallions, corn, and garlic over medium heat for 5 minutes.

Add broth and potato and bring to a simmer. Cook for about 15 minutes or until potato begins to soften.

Add milk, shrimp, asparagus, thyme, and cayenne pepper. Stir and continue to cook for 5 minutes.

Season to taste with salt and black pepper.

MAKES 6 SERVINGS

hot & sour soup

PER SERVING (1 generous cup): 105 calories, 4g fat, 352mg sodium, 10g carbs, 1.5g fiber, 2g sugars, 9g protein

✷ Ingredients

3 cups fat-free chicken broth

14 ounces medium-firm tofu, drained and cut into ¼-inch strips

One 8-ounce can sliced water chestnuts, drained and diced

2 cups whole mushrooms

½ cup chopped scallions

¼ cup egg whites (about 2 egg whites)

¼ cup rice vinegar

1½ tablespoons cornstarch

1 tablespoon light or low-sodium soy sauce

1 teaspoon sesame oil

1 teaspoon minced garlic

1 teaspoon hot chili paste

½ teaspoon black pepper

Optional: additional hot chili paste

✷ Directions

Place mushrooms in a medium bowl and cover them with hot water. Cover the bowl and let stand for 10 minutes, or until mushrooms are tender.

Drain the water from the bowl, dice mushrooms, and set aside.

In a large pot, combine broth with garlic and ¼ cup of water. Bring to a boil. Add mushrooms and water chestnuts, and reduce heat to low. Let simmer for 5 minutes.

Add tofu, rice vinegar, soy sauce, and black pepper. Bring to a boil. Then reduce heat to low and simmer for 10 minutes.

Combine cornstarch with ¼ cup of cold water and stir well, until cornstarch dissolves. Add cornstarch mixture to the broth mixture and bring to a boil. Reduce heat to low. Let simmer for 3 to 5 minutes until thickened, stirring frequently.

Slowly pour egg whites into broth mixture in a steady stream, stirring constantly but gently with a spoon.

Remove from heat and stir in scallions, sesame oil, and chili paste. For super-spicy soup, add more chili paste to taste.

MAKES 6 SERVINGS

CHEW ON THIS:

Wyler's (the bouillon people) once stirred up the World's Largest Bowl of Soup: a 662-gallon bowl of Beef Vegetable!

kazu's special eggplant & shrimp soup

PER SERVING (1 cup): 68 calories, <0.5g fat, 998mg sodium, 9g carbs, 1.5g fiber, 6g sugars, 8g protein

✳✳ *This soup was created by my friend Kazu (the greatest sushi chef on the planet). He serves it at his restaurant in Studio City, California. After eating this soup several times a week for years, I decided it was too delicious to NOT tell the world about it, and I convinced Kazu to share his secret recipe with me. Here it is. Some of the ingredients are a bit hard to find, but PLEASE FIND THEM, AND MAKE THIS SOUP SOON!!!* ✳✳

✳ Ingredients

5 ounces cooked cocktail (medium-small) shrimp

½ cup udon noodle soup base concentrate (found at Japanese markets)

2 cups peeled and cubed eggplant (1-inch cubes), use Japanese eggplant if available

1 fresh Anaheim or banana pepper, deseeded and chopped

1 cup shiitake mushrooms, chopped

✳ Directions

In a medium pot, combine soup base with 3½ cups of water and bring to a boil.

Add all the veggies, reduce heat to low, and simmer for 15 minutes.

Then add the shrimp to the soup. Cook for another 2 minutes or until shrimp are thoroughly heated.

MAKES 5 SERVINGS

HG Tip: *This soup tastes even better the next day (as soups often do!).*

southwestern surprise

PER SERVING (1 generous cup): 168 calories, 1g fat, 702mg sodium, 29g carbs, 6.5g fiber, 6g sugars, 9g protein

✸✸ *Not to sound like a cheesy commercial, but this soup is so thick, it "eats like a meal." It's almost too easy to prepare a super-sized batch, and it tastes even better the next day! (HG Tip: Freeze leftovers in individual servings for microwavable, super-filling, guilt-free snacks!)* ✸✸

✸ Ingredients

4 ounces cooked extra-lean ground beef, drained
One 16-ounce package frozen sweet corn kernels
Two 15-ounce cans pinto beans, rinsed and drained
One 15-ounce can black beans, rinsed and drained
Three 14.5-ounce cans no-salt-added diced tomatoes
One 14.5-ounce can Italian-style diced tomatoes
1 envelope taco seasoning mix
1 envelope ranch dip/dressing mix
¼ cup minced onions
Salt and black pepper, to taste

✸ Directions

Pour the tomatoes and corn into a large pot. Add remaining ingredients and stir thoroughly. Bring to a boil.

Reduce heat to low and let simmer for 15 minutes.

Remove from heat and allow soup to sit for at least 5 minutes. Add salt and pepper to taste.

MAKES 12 SERVINGS

chapter four

four

let's do lunch

lunches and mini meals
it's midday munchie madness!

Are you a mini-meal maniac? Love filling up on lots of
150- to 300-calorie or so eats throughout the day? The
recipes in this chapter are great little snacks or small
meals. There are sandwiches, wraps, kabobs (everything
tastes better on a stick), stir-frys, and more—and all are
awesome. Since this chapter is overflowing with recipes,
let's not waste any time yapping about 'em. Dig in . . .

rockin' tuna melt

PER SERVING (1 sandwich): 212 calories, 2.5g fat, 929mg sodium, 27g carbs, 6g fiber, 7g sugars, 24g protein

✳ Ingredients

2 slices light bread (40 to 45 calories each with about 2g fiber per slice)
2 ounces canned tuna packed in water, drained and flaked
1 tablespoon fat-free mayonnaise
1 tablespoon chopped carrots
1 teaspoon Hellmann's/Best Foods Dijonnaise
1 slice fat-free American cheese
2 slices tomato
Salt and black pepper, to taste

✳ Directions

To make tuna salad, combine tuna, mayo, Dijonnaise, and carrots in a small bowl. Add salt and pepper to taste.

Toast bread slices and then place them on a nonstick baking pan. Pile all of the tuna salad onto one slice of bread. Place tomato on the other slice of bread and cover with cheese.

Place pan in the oven or toaster oven and broil until cheese has melted.

Place the cheese-topped bread slice on top of the tuna-topped slice. Cut sandwich in half and enjoy!

MAKES 1 SERVING

guilt-free 1-2-3 blt

PER SERVING (1 sandwich): 141 calories, 2g fat, 549mg sodium, 22g carbs, 6g fiber, 4g sugars, 11g protein

✴ Ingredients

2 slices light bread (40 to 45 calories each with about 2g fiber per slice)
2 slices (about 1 ounce) extra-lean turkey bacon
2 leaves romaine lettuce
2 slices tomato
2 teaspoons fat-free mayonnaise

✴ Directions

Toast bread. Meanwhile, prepare bacon according to package directions, either in a pan with nonstick spray or in the microwave.

Smear a teaspoon of mayo on each slice of bread. Break bacon slices in half. Top one slice of bread with the bacon, lettuce, and tomato.

Add the other bread slice, cut sandwich in half, and pig out!

MAKES 1 SERVING

HG Tip: *Try it served with a side of pickles. Yummmmmm!*

my big fat greek pita

PER SERVING (2 pita halves): 219 calories, 1.5g fat, 365mg sodium, 43g carbs, 9.5g fiber, 10g sugars, 14g protein

✳ Ingredients

1 whole wheat (or high-fiber) pita
2 ounces fat-free plain Greek yogurt
1 small onion, sliced
½ cup sliced red and green bell peppers
2 cups fresh spinach
½ cup cherry tomatoes, halved
Salt, black pepper, oregano, and garlic powder, to taste
Optional: red pepper flakes

✳ Directions

Cut pita in half and toast, if desired.

In a small dish, combine yogurt with salt, black pepper, oregano, and garlic powder (season to taste). Add red pepper flakes if you want your pita super-spicy.

In a pan sprayed with nonstick spray, cook onion and peppers over medium heat for 5 to 7 minutes.

Add spinach and tomatoes, and cook until spinach wilts.

Remove all veggies from heat and combine with the yogurt sauce. Stuff pita halves with veggie mix.

MAKES 1 SERVING

For a pic of this recipe, see the photo insert. Yay!

bbq-rific chicken wrap

✷✷ *I created this recipe after visiting Memphis (one of my favorite food cities). You'll swear you're eating an authentic pulled chicken BBQ sandwich—slaw 'n all!* ✷✷

✷ Ingredients

1 medium low-fat flour tortilla (about 110 calories with at least 6g fiber)
2½ ounces cooked boneless skinless lean chicken breast, chopped or shredded
⅓ cup prepared coleslaw (packaged or from deli counter)
2 tablespoons barbecue sauce

✷ Directions

Using a strainer, rinse coleslaw until water runs clear (this will remove all the excess fatty mayo but leave in the flavor). Pat slaw dry.

In a bowl, mix chicken, slaw, and barbecue sauce until thoroughly combined. Set aside.

Microwave tortilla until slightly warm. Place chicken mixture in the center of the tortilla.

Wrap tortilla up by folding in the sides first and then rolling it up tightly from the bottom. Place on a plate, seam-side down, and heat in the microwave for an additional 25 seconds.

MAKES 1 SERVING

oatstanding veggie patties

PER SERVING (1 patty): 70 calories, 0.5g fat, 585mg sodium, 16g carbs, 5g fiber, 3g sugars, 4g protein

✶ ✶ *These patties are super-low-cal and high in fiber! And not only are they great for lunch or dinner, they're also perfect for breakfast! BTW, if you accidentally ate all five of these in one sitting (oops!), you'd only take in 350 calories, and you'd down a whopping 25 grams of fiber. Wow!* ✶ ✶

✶ Ingredients

⅓ cup regular oats (not instant)
½ cup Fiber One bran cereal (original)
1 cup diced onions
1 cup diced red and green bell peppers
1 cup diced mushrooms
1 cup diced green beans
¼ cup fat-free liquid egg substitute
2 teaspoons light or low-sodium soy sauce
1 teaspoon salt
¼ teaspoon black pepper
¼ teaspoon garlic powder

✶ Directions

In a blender or food processor, grind Fiber One to a breadcrumb-like consistency. Set aside.

Next, place oats in a small dish. Add about ⅓ cup of boiling water to oats (just enough to cover them) and set aside as well.

In a medium pot sprayed with nonstick spray, cook vegetables for 5 minutes over medium-high heat, stirring occasionally.

Remove pot from heat and transfer veggies, with a slotted spoon, into a large bowl. Allow veggies to cool for several minutes. (If veggies have a lot of excess moisture, use a paper towel to soak it up.)

Add softened oats, ground Fiber One, soy sauce, salt, black pepper, garlic powder, and egg substitute to veggies. Stir thoroughly to combine. Make sure mixture is well blended.

Form mixture tightly into 5 balls and place them on a large plate. Cover and allow to cool and set in the fridge for several hours. (The longer they sit in the fridge, the better they'll keep their shape when you cook 'em.) Don't worry if they are a little bit watery—they'll firm up when cooking.

Using a spatula, flatten them into patties in a pan sprayed with nonstick spray and cook for about 5 minutes per side over medium heat (flip gently, so they keep their shape).

MAKES 5 SERVINGS

HG Tip: *Load 'em up with your favorite burger condiments like pickles, ketchup, and mustard.*

For Weight Watchers *POINTS*® values and photos of all the recipes in this book, check out hungry-girl.com/book.

veggie tuna wrap explosion

PER SERVING (1 wrap): 215 calories, 3.5g fat, 886mg sodium, 30g carbs, 10g fiber, 5g sugars, 21g protein

✷ Ingredients

1 medium low-fat flour tortilla (about 110 calories with at least 6g fiber)
2 ounces canned tuna (packed in water), drained and flaked
2 tablespoons broccoli coleslaw mix (or regular slaw mix), dry
1 tablespoon chopped dill pickle
1 tablespoon chopped red onions
2 small tomato slices, halved
1 tablespoon fat-free mayonnaise
2 teaspoons Hellmann's/Best Foods Dijonnaise

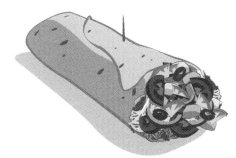

✷ Directions

Microwave tortilla until slightly warm. Set aside.

Combine tuna, mayo, and Dijonnaise. Add pickle, onions, and slaw. Mix well.

Place tuna mixture in the center of your tortilla. Add tomato slices, then fold in tortilla sides and roll it up tightly. Enjoy!

MAKES 1 SERVING

HG SANDWICH SHOCKER!

Think the average tuna sandwich is your best bet for a light lunch? Sorry, Charlie! Our fishy friend from the sea is often swimming in fat-filled mayo. A tuna salad sandwich can actually have more calories than a 12-ounce filet mignon. Eeeek!

Your Office = Your Gym?

No time to head out for a workout? Turn simple office staples (as in common items, not the pointy metal pieces used to secure documents!) into an at-work gym. Try doing a few of these fun fitness drills periodically throughout the day . . .

Cardio Quickies: Walk some stairs in your office building for 5 minutes (if there are no stairs, walk around the office at a quick pace). For a heart-pumping challenge, take stairs two at a time.

Chair Squats: While sitting, lift your butt off the seat and hover over your chair for 2 to 3 seconds. Stand up and then repeat.

Chair Dips: Make sure your chair is stable. Place your hands on the chair, next to your hips. Walk your feet out and move your hips in front of your chair, and bend your elbows, lowering your body until your elbows are at a 90-degree angle. Return to starting position and repeat.

Ab Recliners: Again, be sure your chair is stable. Sit on the edge of your chair, arms extended in front. Keeping your back straight, contract your abs and slowly lower your torso toward the back of your chair. Hold for 2 to 3 seconds, and then slowly return to starting position. Repeat.

Core Curls: Cross your arms over your chest and sit up straight. Contract your abs and curl your shoulders toward your hips, pulling abs in. Hold for 2 seconds, return to start and repeat.

crab-ulous smothered burrito

PER SERVING (1 burrito): 300 calories, 4.5g fat, 1,472mg sodium, 47g carbs, 13.5g fiber, 4g sugars, 25g protein

✳ Ingredients

1 medium low-fat flour tortilla (about 110 calories with at least 6g fiber)
2 ounces drained white crabmeat
1 cup broccoli florets
¼ cup canned black beans
¼ cup green enchilada sauce
2 tablespoons fat-free cream cheese
2 tablespoons fat-free sour cream
¼ teaspoon lemon pepper seasoning
½ teaspoon parsley
Optional topping: additional fat-free sour cream

✳ Directions

Preheat oven to 375 degrees.

Place broccoli in a microwave-safe bowl with 1 tablespoon of water. Cover and microwave for 3 minutes. Drain any remaining water and set aside.

Microwave tortilla until slightly warm.

Combine crabmeat, cream cheese, sour cream, parsley, and lemon pepper seasoning. Place crab mixture in the center of the tortilla. Top with broccoli and black beans.

Roll tortilla up tightly and place seam-side down on a baking dish sprayed lightly with nonstick spray.

Place dish in the oven and cook for 10 minutes or until insides are thoroughly heated and tortilla is slightly toasty. Meanwhile, warm the enchilada sauce in the microwave for 8 to 10 seconds.

Remove burrito and cover with sauce. Top with fat-free sour cream, if desired.

MAKES 1 SERVING

HG Tip: Save around 300mg of sodium by skipping the sauce and enjoying your burrito NAKED (the burrito—you can actually wear clothes).

CHEW ON THIS:

If you spend 5 minutes out of every hour of your workday running in place, climbing stairs, or doing squats, lunges, and arm raises, by the end of the day you'll have worked out for 40 minutes!

too-good turkey club wrap

PER SERVING (1 wrap): 275 calories, 4g fat, 1,035mg sodium, 29g carbs, 9.5g fiber, 6g sugars, 35g protein

✴ Ingredients

1 medium low-fat flour tortilla (about 110 calories with at least 6g fiber)
2 ounces cooked skinless lean turkey breast, chopped
2 slices (about 1 ounce) extra-lean turkey bacon
1 slice fat-free American cheese
2 leaves romaine lettuce
2 tablespoons diced tomatoes
5 cucumber slices
1 tablespoon fat-free mayonnaise

✴ Directions

Over medium heat, cook bacon strips in a pan sprayed with nonstick spray until crispy (about 5 minutes). Once cool enough to handle, chop bacon into small pieces.

Combine turkey, bacon, mayo, and tomatoes in a small bowl. Mix thoroughly.

Microwave tortilla until slightly warm. Lay the tortilla out on a piece of foil (a little larger than the tortilla) with about a 2-inch section of the tortilla extending over the foil.

Tear lettuce into bite-sized pieces. Place cheese, lettuce, cucumber slices, and turkey mixture into the center of the tortilla.

Fold the right side of the tortilla in at a diagonal. Then fold the left side in at a diagonal. Flip the bottom up to prevent the contents from falling out. Wrap the foil around the tortilla in the same manner. The end result will be a waffle-cone-style wrap!

MAKES 1 SERVING

HG Tip: You can easily enjoy this wrap without the tortilla! Instead of tearing the lettuce leaves into bite-sized pieces, use them as the outer part of the wrap. You can wrap the foil around the leaves the same way as in the tortilla version. The Turkey Club Lettuce Wrap comes in at about 145 calories, and it rocks!

For a pic of this recipe, see the photo insert. Yay!

· ·

Wrap It Up Right! A Tortilla Tutorial

Everything you need to know to succeed in the wonderful world of wraps . . .

Step 1: Slightly warm your tortilla by microwaving it for about 10 seconds. Doing so will make it easier to work with, and it'll also taste better.

Step 2: Place your stuff in the center of your tortilla. First fold the sides in (a few inches), and then fold the bottom to the center, creating an envelope around your filling. Use a fork to smoosh any attempted escapees into the pocket you've created.

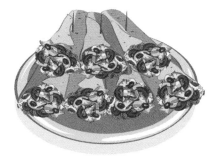

Step 3: Slowly roll your tortilla upward until you reach the top. Voilà!

yummilicious veggie burger wrap

PER SERVING (1 wrap): 253 calories, 6.5g fat, 941mg sodium, 35g carbs, 13g fiber, 4g sugars, 18g protein

✴ Ingredients

1 medium low-fat flour tortilla (about 110 calories with at least 6g fiber)
1 veggie burger patty (veggie-based rather than the imitation-meat kind)
1 wedge The Laughing Cow Light Original Swiss cheese
3 tablespoons chopped mushrooms
1 tablespoon chopped onions
Optional condiments: ketchup, mustard, fat-free mayonnaise, salsa

✴ Directions

Microwave tortilla until slightly warm. Lay the tortilla out and spread the cheese wedge evenly on top of it.

In a pan sprayed with nonstick spray, cook the veggie patty over medium heat. (Refer to the package for exact cooking time.) Once patty is half-cooked, remove it from the pan and chop into bite-sized pieces.

Place the onions and patty pieces in the pan and continue cooking for 1 minute. Then add mushrooms, stir, and cook for 2 additional minutes or until veggies are fully cooked.

Remove pan from heat and allow to cool slightly. Evenly spoon mixture into the center of the cheese-covered tortilla. If desired, top with guilt-free condiments.

Fold in the sides of the tortilla and roll it up. Place on a microwave-safe plate, seam-side down, and heat for 30 seconds.

MAKES 1 SERVING

veggie-friendly
asian lettuce wraps

PER SERVING (3 wraps): 220 calories, 3.5g fat, 971mg sodium, 30g carbs, 8g fiber, 10g sugars, 21g protein

★ Ingredients

6 medium iceberg lettuce leaves (or leaves from another round, firm head of lettuce)
6 ounces ground-beef-style soy crumbles, defrosted if previously frozen
1 cup canned sliced water chestnuts, drained and chopped
¾ cup chopped shiitake mushrooms
1 cup bean sprouts
½ cup chopped scallions
2 tablespoons light or low-sodium soy sauce
1 tablespoon dark brown sugar (not packed)
2 teaspoons chili garlic sauce (found in the Asian foods aisle)
½ teaspoon sesame oil

★ Directions

Combine soy sauce, sugar, garlic sauce, and sesame oil in a small dish. Mix well and set aside.

Bring a medium pot sprayed with nonstick spray to medium heat. Place all ingredients, except for the scallions and lettuce leaves, into the pot. Add the prepared sauce and stir. Cook for 2 to 3 minutes.

Add scallions, cook for 1 minute more and remove from heat.

Divide mixture evenly among the 6 lettuce "cups" and enjoy.

MAKES 2 SERVINGS

weeeee . . . veggie wheels!

PER SERVING (6 pieces): 143 calories, 2.5g fat, 506mg sodium, 27g carbs, 10g fiber, 3g sugars, 10g protein

✴ Ingredients

1 medium low-fat flour tortilla (about 110 calories with at least 6g fiber)
¼ cup chopped red bell peppers
½ cup fresh spinach (stems removed)
1 tablespoon chopped tomatoes
1 tablespoon chopped scallions
1 tablespoon fat-free cream cheese
¼ teaspoon ranch seasoning mix, dry

✴ Directions

In a small bowl, combine cream cheese and ranch seasoning until smooth and mixed thoroughly.

Microwave tortilla until slightly warm. Lay the tortilla on a flat surface and evenly spread cream cheese mixture on top of it.

Place spinach, red peppers, scallions, and tomatoes evenly over cheese layer. Very tightly roll the tortilla up from one end to the other, creating a pinwheel of layers, as opposed to a burrito. Wrap the tortilla securely in plastic wrap and place it in the fridge for at least 1 hour.

When you're ready to eat, remove the plastic wrap and cut off both ends of the wrap (where the tortilla does not fully wrap around). Slice the rest of the wrap into 6 circular pieces. Enjoy!

MAKES 1 SERVING

HG Tip: Try making a bunch of these cute rolls, and put together a big tray for your next party. They'll be a hit!

More Tips 'n Tricks for Burning Calories at the Office!

Remember, the more calories you burn, the more HG recipes you can enjoy . . .

* **Use the restroom on a different floor and take the stairs to get there.**

* **Walk as much as possible—hand-deliver documents and visit people in their offices down the hall instead of calling them.**

* **Set your cell phone alarm to go off every few hours to remind you to walk around a little bit—get moving!**

rockin' shrimp pad thai

PER SERVING (½ of recipe): 242 calories, 3g fat, 1,101mg sodium, 29g carbs, 9g fiber, 11g sugars, 27g protein

✶✶ *This Pad Thai is as good as any I've ever tasted—and it is insanely low in fat and calories compared to the real thing!* ✶✶

✶ Ingredients

Never worked with Tofu Shirataki before? Turn to page 261 for helpful hints!

2 packages House Foods Tofu Shirataki, Fettuccine Shape

4 ounces cooked medium shrimp

2 cups chopped broccoli

1½ cups bean sprouts

¾ cup chopped scallions

½ cup fat-free liquid egg substitute

2 tablespoons canned tomato sauce

2 tablespoons light or low-sodium teriyaki sauce

1 tablespoon chili garlic sauce (found in the Asian foods aisle)

1 teaspoon reduced-fat peanut butter

2 tablespoons Splenda No Calorie Sweetener (granulated)

✶ Directions

Rinse and drain shirataki noodles well. Pat dry. Place noodles in a microwave-safe bowl and microwave for 1 minute.

Drain excess liquid from noodles and pat them until thoroughly dry. Cut noodles into pieces about 3 inches in length. Set aside.

In a small bowl, combine tomato sauce, teriyaki sauce, chili garlic sauce, peanut butter, and Splenda, and stir thoroughly. Set aside, as well.

Spray a wok or large pan with nonstick spray and set heat to medium-high. Once pan is hot, add egg substitute. Stirring constantly, cook for 1 minute or until egg is soft-scrambled.

Add broccoli, sprouts, and scallions, and cook for 2 minutes. Then add noodles, sauce mixture, and shrimp. Stir thoroughly, and cook for 3 minutes or until dish is heated throughout.

MAKES 2 SERVINGS

HG Tip!

Find yourself starved by dinnertime if you eat lunch early, but notice your stomach's growling all morning if you wait 'til late afternoon? Split your lunch up into two mini meals for all-day energy and ultimate satisfaction.

mexi-tato

✳ Ingredients

1 medium (8-ounce) baking potato
2 tablespoons fat-free liquid non-dairy creamer
2 tablespoons shredded fat-free cheddar cheese
¼ cup canned black beans
½ teaspoon taco seasoning mix, dry
2 tablespoons chopped tomatoes
1 tablespoon chopped scallions
Dash of salt
Dash of black pepper
Optional topping: fat-free sour cream

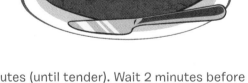

✳ Directions

Pierce potato in several places with a fork. Next, peel the skin off of the top of the potato only. Place potato, peeled side up, in the microwave and cook for 6 to 8 minutes (until tender). Wait 2 minutes before removing potato from the microwave.

Gently remove all of the pulp from the potato and place it in a microwave-safe dish. Set the empty shell aside. Add the creamer, cheese, taco seasoning, salt, and black pepper to the potato pulp and stir. Microwave mixture for 45 seconds and stir again.

Next, heat black beans in the microwave.

Place half of the cheesy potato mixture in the potato shell and then top with half of the black beans. Repeat.

Top potato with tomatoes and scallions and, if desired, sour cream. Dig in!

MAKES 1 SERVING

TOP ATE Fatty, High-Cal Sandwich Disasters
It's sandwich insanity . . .

1. Tuna Melt (800 calories and 50g fat!)
2. Bacon Cheeseburger (775 calories and 45g fat!)
3. Reuben (750 calories and 40g fat!)
4. Meatball Sub (675 calories and 30g fat!)
5. Turkey Club (700 calories and 35g fat!)
6. Grilled Cheese (650 calories and 45g fat!)
7. Fried Fish Sandwich (600 calories and 30g fat!)
8. Philly Cheesesteak (750 calories and 35g fat!)

Nutritional information based on averages.

saucy bbq seafood skewers

✳ Ingredients

For Skewers

4 ounces raw Atlantic salmon

4 ounces large raw peeled and deveined shrimp, tails removed

6 ounces large raw sea scallops

8 to 10 cherry tomatoes

1 medium-large zucchini

For Sauce

¼ cup canned tomato sauce

2 tablespoons ketchup

2 teaspoons brown sugar (not packed)

2 teaspoons cider vinegar

½ teaspoon garlic powder

✳ Directions

Cut scallops into halves or quarters, depending on their size, so that they are just slightly larger than the shrimp. Cut salmon and zucchini into chunks about the same size as the scallops.

Place all veggies and seafood onto 4 skewers, alternating the order.

Combine sauce ingredients in a small dish. Set aside.

Place skewers on a grill or in a large hot pan sprayed with nonstick spray. Cook skewers at medium heat for about 5 minutes or until seafood just begins to turn opaque on top.

Flip skewers and cook for an additional 4 to 5 minutes or until all seafood is cooked throughout. While skewers cook, warm sauce in the microwave.

Drizzle or brush sauce over skewers immediately after removing them from heat.

MAKES 2 SERVINGS

What About Kabob?

Get skewer savvy NOW!

✱ Always leave at least 1 inch of space on both ends of each skewer. This will make them easier to handle and flip.

✱ If using wooden skewers, soak them for 20 minutes in water to prevent burning.

✱ When whipping up your own kabob creations, pair foods on skewers based on their cooking times. Shrimp, scallops, mushrooms, and tomatoes all cook pretty quickly. Chicken, steak, onions, and potatoes all take longer. Or, slightly steam-cook the foods that take longest to grill before you skewer 'em. That way you can throw everything on to cook at once without worry!

✱ For a fun twist, soak wooden skewers in your favorite non-oil-based liquid, like orange juice, balsamic vinegar, or soy sauce. This will season your kabobs from the inside out, while adding barely any calories or fat!

✱ Mix it up! Toss some fruit chunks on your kabobs and you'll satisfy your sweet tooth before you finish your meal! Tough, firm fruits like pineapple, mango, melon, and pear work best.

citrus-y stir-fry shrimp

✶ Ingredients

10 ounces raw peeled and deveined shrimp, tails removed

3 cups snow peas

3 cups white mushrooms, quartered

½ cup canned sliced water chestnuts, drained and halved

⅓ cup freshly squeezed orange juice (straight from the fruit, no cheating!)

½ teaspoon cornstarch

2½ teaspoons Splenda No Calorie Sweetener (granulated)

3 tablespoons light or low-sodium soy sauce

2½ teaspoons minced garlic

Optional: 2 tablespoons chopped scallions

✶ Directions

Bring a medium pot filled two-thirds of the way with water to a boil.

Meanwhile, in a small dish, combine orange juice, soy sauce, Splenda, cornstarch, and garlic (if using scallions, add those as well). Mix thoroughly and transfer to a small saucepan. Set heat to low and cook for 5 minutes, stirring often.

Remove sauce from heat, transfer back to the small dish, and set aside.

Once the pot of water has reached a full boil, add shrimp. Cook until shrimp are opaque (about 35 seconds for large shrimp). Drain water, and rinse shrimp in cold water and set aside.

In a large pot or wok sprayed with nonstick spray, cook snow peas and mushrooms at medium heat, stirring occasionally, for 5 to 7 minutes. (Veggies should still be crisp.)

Add shrimp, water chestnuts, and sauce. Stir and continue to cook for 2 to 3 more minutes, until entire dish is thoroughly heated and mixed.

MAKES 2 SERVINGS

HG Tip: To make juicing an orange easier (if you don't have a fancy juicer), roll the fruit around on the counter before cutting it.

CHEW ON THIS:

People who eat their biggest meal of the day at lunchtime tend not to overindulge in the evening, which keeps those late-night snacking pounds from packing on.

loaded 'n oated veggie pizza

PER SERVING (1 pizza): 231 calories, 2g fat, 870mg sodium,
37g carbs, 11g fiber, 6g sugars, 24g protein

✷✷ *The Fiber One 'n oat crust is definitely unique—and it makes this pizza crazy-high in fiber and slightly sweet!* ✷✷

✶ Ingredients

¼ cup Fiber One bran cereal (original)
¼ cup regular oats (not instant)
¼ cup fat-free liquid egg substitute
⅓ cup shredded fat-free mozzarella cheese
1 tablespoon diced mushrooms
1 tablespoon diced green bell peppers
1 tablespoon diced onions
⅓ cup canned tomato sauce
½ teaspoon garlic powder
Optional: salt, black pepper, oregano, additional garlic powder, onion powder, red
     pepper flakes, etc.

✶ Directions

Preheat oven to 400 degrees.

Place oats and Fiber One in a blender or food processor and grind until a breadcrumb-like consistency is reached. In a small bowl, combine the "breadcrumb" mixture, egg substitute, and garlic powder. Mix well.

Over medium-high heat, spoon mixture into a pan sprayed with nonstick spray and smooth into a circular shape (larger for a thin crust, smaller for a thick crust). Allow to cook until the bottom is slightly browned (about 2 minutes) and then gently flip. Once both sides are slightly browned, remove crust from the pan and place it on a plate to cool.

Remove pan from heat and respray. Cook diced veggies in the pan over medium-high heat for 1 to 2 minutes. Remove from heat.

Season tomato sauce, to taste, with any of the optional ingredients and mix well. Pour sauce evenly onto the oat/cereal crust.

Next, evenly top crust—first with the cheese and then with the veggies. Place pizza directly on the oven rack and cook for 10 minutes.

If you like, season your pizza with more optional ingredients. Cut into quarters for four times the fun!

MAKES 1 SERVING

 For a pic of this recipe, see the photo insert. Yay!

For Weight Watchers **POINTS**®
values and photos of all the
recipes in this book, check out
hungry-girl.com/book.

hawaiian pineapple chicken skewers

PER SERVING (2 skewers): 178 calories, 1.5g fat, 751mg sodium, 19g carbs, 2.5g fiber, 12g sugars, 23g protein

✴ Ingredients

½ cup pineapple juice
6 ounces raw boneless skinless lean chicken breast
4 medium white mushrooms
½ medium onion, cut into 8 slices
½ medium yellow bell pepper, cut into 4 slices
½ medium red bell pepper, cut into 4 slices
½ medium green bell pepper, cut into 4 slices
½ cup pineapple (4 chunks)
2 tablespoons teriyaki sauce

✴ Directions

Cut the chicken breast into 12 chunks. Place them in a small bowl and then cover with pineapple juice. Cover the bowl and let chicken marinate in the fridge for at least 30 minutes.

Once the chicken has marinated, drain the pineapple juice from the bowl. Evenly distribute the chicken, pineapple, and veggies among 4 skewers. Suggested stacking per skewer: 1 slice onion, 1 slice green pepper, 1 chicken chunk, 1 pineapple

chunk, 1 chicken chunk, 1 slice yellow pepper, 1 mushroom, 1 chicken chunk, 1 slice red pepper, 1 slice onion.

In a large pan sprayed with nonstick spray, cook kabobs over medium-high heat for about 10 minutes, flipping halfway, or until desired texture is reached and chicken is cooked thoroughly.

Drizzle with teriyaki sauce immediately before serving.

MAKES 2 SERVINGS

HG Tip: *Feel free to use an indoor or outdoor grill for cooking these skewers instead. Just make sure the chicken is fully cooked before chowing down!*

chapter five

junk food junkie

fast-food makeovers
ditch the drive-thru. pig out at home.

Americans spend over 120 billion dollars on fast food every year (probably because it tastes good and is convenient). Well, the swaps in this chapter are not only delicious, they're also *easy* to make. And making better-for-you junk food is *really* fun (yeah, we're dorks!). There's nothing quite like that "Eureka!" feeling you get when you discover a *brilliant* way to turn some high-cal, fatty dish into something healthy. This chapter contains a bunch of recipes that feature HG's famous Fiber One "bread-crumbs." They can literally help you turn almost any deep-fried item into something baked, crunchy, and good for you. You'll also find guilt-free swaps for nachos, fries, giant burgers, pizza, and more . . .

hg's famous bowl

PER SERVING (1 bowl): 288 calories, 6.5g fat, 967mg sodium, 43g carbs, 5g fiber, 7g sugars, 18g protein

✴ Ingredients

1 breaded-chicken-style soy patty
1 cup peeled and cubed butternut squash
¼ cup fat-free chicken gravy, heated
1 ounce fat-free milk
2 tablespoons canned sweet corn kernels, heated
2 tablespoons shredded fat-free cheese (cheddar or American)
Salt and black pepper, to taste

For the 411 on getting perfectly cubed squash, take a peek at "Butternut Squash Basics" on page 279!

✴ Directions

In a covered dish, microwave butternut squash pieces with ¼ cup of water for 4 to 6 minutes or until tender. Drain excess water and then mash squash with the milk. Season to taste with salt and black pepper.

Place mashed squash in a medium bowl. Next, sprinkle corn over the squash.

Prepare "chicken" patty according to package directions, in the microwave or in a pan with nonstick spray, and then cut into small pieces.

Place patty pieces on top of the corn-topped squash. Drizzle with gravy. Top with shredded cheese and enjoy!

MAKES 1 SERVING

ooey-gooey chili cheese nachos

✶✶ *These nachos are soooo good. And the cheese sauce can be used in tons of other recipes, too. Don't forget that!* ✶✶

✶ Ingredients

One 7-ounce bag baked tortilla chips
1 cup low-fat turkey or veggie chili
¾ cup salsa
½ cup light soymilk
3 ounces fat-free block cheddar cheese
1 wedge The Laughing Cow Light Original Swiss cheese
2 tablespoons fat-free cream cheese
2 tablespoons fat-free sour cream

✶ Directions

Place all three cheeses in a saucepan with the soymilk. Heat over low heat, stirring occasionally. Continue until all cheeses have melted and your cheese sauce is thoroughly mixed and hot.

Prepare chili according to package directions. Microwave chips in a bowl until warm and then spread them out on a large platter.

Pour your cheese sauce over the chips. Top with chili. Spoon salsa and sour cream on top and, voilà, your nachos are ready!

MAKES 6 SERVINGS

For a pic of this recipe, see the photo insert. Yay!

bake-tastic butternut squash fries

PER SERVING (½ of recipe): 125 calories, <0.5g fat, 158mg sodium, 33g carbs, 3g fiber, 6g sugars, 3g protein

✱✱ *Warning: You may become addicted to these fries and find yourself making them daily once you try 'em!* ✱✱

✱ Ingredients

1 medium butternut squash (about 2 pounds—
    large enough to yield 20 ounces uncooked flesh)
⅛ teaspoon kosher salt

✱ Directions

Preheat oven to 425 degrees.

Use a sharp knife to remove the ends of the squash. Cut squash in half widthwise (making it easier to manage) and then peel squash halves using a vegetable peeler or a knife. Cut squash in half lengthwise and then scoop out all seeds.

Next, cut squash into French fry shapes. Use a crinkle cutter to make authentic-looking crinkle-cut fries (they'll taste great any way you slice 'em, though). Using a paper towel, pat squash pieces firmly to absorb any excess moisture.

Place squash in a bowl, add a light mist of nonstick spray, and sprinkle with salt. Toss squash to evenly distribute salt and then transfer to a large baking pan sprayed with nonstick spray. Use 2 pans if needed. Squash pieces should lie flat in the pan.

Place pan(s) in the oven and bake for 40 minutes or so (longer for thick-cut fries, shorter for skinnier fries), flipping halfway through baking. Fries are done when they are starting to brown on the edges and get crispy.

MAKES 2 SERVINGS

HG Tip: Serve with ketchup, mustard, sugar-free maple syrup, or however else you enjoy regular fries or sweet potato fries!

For b-nut squash cooking tips (and more squash-tastic recipes), visit the butternut squash section of the "Fun With . . ." chapter on page 276!

HG SHOCKER!

An average 6-ounce serving of French fries contains about 500 calories and 25 grams of fat. But a 6-ounce potato only contains about 130 calories and virtually no fat. That means when you order up those fries, you're ingesting more than 350 calories and about 25 fat grams of pure oil! Eww . . .

super-skinny skins

PER SERVING (4 pieces): 157 calories, 1g fat, 271mg sodium, 28g carbs, 4.5g fiber, 1g sugars, 10g protein

✳ Ingredients

3 medium (8-ounce) baking potatoes
½ cup shredded fat-free cheddar cheese
2 tablespoons imitation bacon bits
Optional toppings: chopped scallions, fat-free sour cream, salsa

✳ Directions

Preheat oven to 375 degrees.

Pierce potatoes several times with a fork. Place potatoes on a microwave-safe plate. Microwave for 4 minutes.

Turn potatoes over and return them to microwave for 4 more minutes. Allow them to cool for a few minutes.

Cut potatoes in half lengthwise. Using a fork, gently scrape out the bulk of the flesh. Place the empty potato shells on a baking dish spritzed with nonstick spray. Place dish in the oven and cook for 8 to 10 minutes, depending on how crispy you like your potato skins.

Evenly distribute cheese and bacon bits on top of potato skins. Return skins to the oven until the cheese has melted.

Cut each potato skin in half. If desired, top with scallions and serve with sour cream and/or salsa.

MAKES 3 SERVINGS

Junk Food Face Off!

In this corner . . .

Onion Rings vs. French Fries
1 medium order of onion rings (about 4.5 ounces) = 450 calories and 25g fat
1 medium order of French fries (about 5 ounces) = 415 calories and 19g fat

Ounce for ounce, onion rings have about 20 percent more calories than French fries and nearly 35 percent more fat!!!!

Milkshake vs. Ice Cream Float
1 vanilla milkshake = 670 calories and 27g fat
1 ice cream float made with vanilla ice cream = 360 calories and 14g fat

An ice cream float clocks in with 310 fewer calories and saves you 13 grams of fat! Order it made with diet soda instead of regular and you'll save another 140 calories!

Hamburger vs. Fish Sandwich
1 fast-food regular hamburger = 280 calories and 10g fat
1 fast-food fried fish sandwich = 500 calories and 23g fat

Surprise . . . That fishy fried sandwich contains more than twice the fat of the burger, and it's loaded with a lot more calories, too!

Pretzels vs. Potato Chips
1 ounce pretzels = 110 calories and 1g fat
1 ounce potato chips = 155 calories and 10g fat

Choosing chips over pretzels can be a fat-astrophe, as chips typically have *ten times* as much fat!

Nutritional information based on averages.

lord of the onion rings

PER SERVING (entire recipe): 153 calories, 1g fat, 379mg sodium, 41g carbs, 16g fiber, 7g sugars, 9g protein

✳ ✳ *Using Fiber One as a low-cal, high-fiber way to fake-fry is one of the greatest ideas I've ever had. I roll pretty much everything in F1 "breadcrumbs" and bake it. IT ROCKS!!!* ✳ ✳

✳ Ingredients

For the 411 on faux-frying with Fiber One, see page 113!

1 large onion
½ cup Fiber One bran cereal (original)
¼ cup fat-free liquid egg substitute
Dash of salt
Optional: additional salt, black pepper, oregano, garlic powder,
    onion powder, etc.

✳ Directions

Preheat oven to 375 degrees.

Cut the ends off of the onion, and remove the outer layer. Cut onion into ½-inch-wide slices, and separate into rings.

Using a blender or food processor, grind Fiber One to a breadcrumb-like consistency. Pour Fiber One "breadcrumbs" into a small dish and mix in salt, and any optional spices you like.

Next, fill a small bowl (just large enough for onion rings to fit in) with egg substitute. One by one, coat each ring first in egg and then in the "breadcrumbs" (give each ring a shake after the egg bath).

Evenly place rings on a baking dish sprayed with nonstick spray. Cook for 20 to 25 minutes, flipping rings over about halfway through.

MAKES 1 HUMONGOUS SERVING

📷 For a pic of this recipe, see the photo insert. Yay!

· ·

CHEW ON THIS:

An average order of onion rings at a fast-food joint contains 450 calories and 25 grams of fat. An average onion contains 50 calories and no fat.

big bopper burger stopper

PER SERVING (1 sandwich): 202 calories, 2.5g fat, 789mg sodium, 32g carbs, 6g fiber, 6g sugars, 17g protein

✳ Ingredients

1 small hamburger bun (light, if available)
1 Boca Meatless Burger, Original
3 slices/chips dill pickle
1 slice tomato
1 leaf romaine lettuce
1 slice onion
1 teaspoon fat-free mayonnaise
1 teaspoon ketchup

✳ Directions

Prepare patty per package instructions, using nonstick spray or nothing at all. Toast bun, if desired.

Place patty on the bun's bottom half and then top with tomato, onion, lettuce, and pickle slices.

On the top half of the bun, smear on mayo and ketchup. Put two halves together and enjoy!

MAKES 1 SERVING

HG Alternative: *Love cheese? Slap a slice of fat-free American on the bottom half of your bun. The cheesed-up version has just 233 calories!*

 For a pic of this recipe, see the photo insert. Yay!

TOP ATE Drive-Thru Disasters

Drive right past these calorie-clogged, fat-happy food freaks . . .

1. Burger King Whopper w/Cheese (990 calories and 64g fat!)

2. Dairy Queen 6-piece Chicken Strip Basket w/BBQ Hot Dip (1,330 calories and 61g fat!)

3. Jack in the Box Ultimate Cheeseburger (1,010 calories and 71g fat!)

4. Carl's Jr. Double Western Bacon Cheeseburger (970 calories and 53g fat!)

5. Dairy Queen ½ lb. FlameThrower GrillBurger (1,030 calories and 73g fat!)

6. Arby's Classic Italian Toasted Sub (827 calories and 45g fat!)

7. Taco Bell Grilled Stuft Burrito (680 calories and 30g fat!)

8. Hardee's Monster Thickburger (1,410 calories and 107g fat!)

perfect pepperoni pizzas

PER SERVING (2 mini pizzas): 190 calories, 3g fat,
859mg sodium, 25g carbs, 6.5g fiber, 2g sugars, 20g protein

✳✳ *Try chopping the pepperoni up into mini pieces. That way you'll feel like you're devouring 2 little pizza pies loaded with pepperoni!* ✳✳

✳ Ingredients

1 light English muffin
¼ cup shredded fat-free mozzarella cheese
8 pieces (about ½ ounce) turkey pepperoni
2 tablespoons canned tomato sauce
Optional: salt, black pepper, oregano, garlic powder, onion powder,
      red pepper flakes, etc.

✳ Directions

Preheat oven to 350 degrees.

Season tomato sauce, to taste, with any of the optional ingredients. Split English muffin in half and spread sauce on both halves.

Evenly sprinkle cheese over the 2 halves and then top with pepperoni. Place muffin halves on a baking pan sprayed lightly with nonstick spray and cook for 12 to 14 minutes.

Season as you would a regular slice of pie!

MAKES 1 SERVING

Slim Down Your Pizza Slice!

How to handle the real deal . . .

* Order it cheese-less (if you dare!).

* Choose thin crust instead of thick and you'll save countless calories per slice!

* Blot your pizza before chomping into it and you'll eliminate dozens of calories and plenty of fat.

* Opt for veggie toppings instead of meats (and no, fried eggplant doesn't count!).

CHEW ON THIS:

Most fast-food restaurants have menus and nutritional information on their websites, so check those out and decide what you want before you go. Arming yourself with information is key to making good food choices.

swapcorn shrimp

PER SERVING (entire recipe): 180 calories, 2.5g fat, 346mg sodium, 27g carbs, 14g fiber, 0g sugars, 25g protein

✶✶ *These are fantastic eaten alone, with ketchup, or with a little cocktail sauce!* ✶✶

✶ Ingredients

3 ounces raw peeled and deveined shrimp, tails removed
½ cup Fiber One bran cereal (original)
¼ cup fat-free liquid egg substitute
Salt and black pepper, to taste

For the 411 on faux-frying with Fiber One, see page 113!

✶ Directions

Preheat oven to 350 degrees.

Pour egg substitute into a bowl and set aside.

Using a blender or food processor, grind Fiber One cereal to a breadcrumb-like consistency. Pour crumbs into a plastic container that has an airtight lid (or into a sealable plastic bag). Add as much salt and black pepper as you like to the crumbs.

Make sure shrimp are as dry as possible (use a paper towel to soak up moisture). Place them in the dish with egg substitute and coat them thoroughly. Transfer shrimp to Fiber One container or bag and secure lid or seal bag. Then shake until shrimp are well coated.

Place shrimp on a baking dish sprayed with nonstick spray. Cook shrimp for 15 to 20 minutes, flipping them about halfway through, until outsides are crispy.

MAKES 1 SERVING

hot diggity chili dog

PER SERVING (1 chili dog): 109 calories, 1g fat, 632mg sodium, 17g carbs, 3.5g fiber, 3g sugars, 10g protein

✷✷ *Guilt-free chili dogs . . . YES!!!!* ✷✷

✶ Ingredients

1 fat-free or nearly fat-free hot dog (40 to 50 calories)
1 slice light bread (40 to 45 calories with about 2g fiber)
2 tablespoons low-fat turkey or veggie chili

✶ Directions

Prepare the hot dog and chili according to package directions.

Place hot dog in the center of the bread slice and fold bread sides up around the dog.

Top with chili and, voilà, you have your *awesome* chili dog!

MAKES 1 SERVING

For Weight Watchers *POINTS*® values and photos of all the recipes in this book, check out hungry-girl.com/book.

fiber-ific fried chicken strips

PER SERVING (8 strips): 277 calories, 3g fat, 696mg sodium, 26g carbs, 14g fiber, 0g sugars, 47g protein

✴✴ Trust me, these chicken strips will quickly become a staple in your diet. (The serving size is huge, so feel free to save some for later!) ✴✴

✴ Ingredients

6 ounces raw skinless boneless lean chicken breast, cut into 8 strips
½ cup Fiber One bran cereal (original)
¼ cup fat-free liquid egg substitute
¼ teaspoon garlic salt
Black pepper, to taste

✴ Directions

Preheat oven to 375 degrees.

Using a blender or food processor, grind Fiber One to a breadcrumb-like consistency. Add garlic salt and black pepper to crumbs. Place crumbs in one small dish and egg substitute in another.

Next, coat raw chicken—first with egg and then with crumbs. Place strips on a baking pan sprayed with nonstick spray. Add a light mist of nonstick spray on top and place in the oven.

Cook for 10 minutes and then turn strips over. Spritz with another light mist of nonstick spray and cook for an additional 7 to 10 minutes, until chicken is fully cooked and crumb coating looks crispy. Enjoy!

MAKES 1 SERVING

Secrets of Fiber-Frying!
The Fiber One Breadcrumb Breakdown

Master HG's recipes, and even create a few of your own . . .

✱ Have some fun with these recipes by swapping out the egg substitute (which merely helps the crumb coating stick to the chicken) with things like hot sauce, barbecue sauce, or fat-free salad dressings. Your food will pick up some flavor but not a lot of calories!

✱ Although you'll only actually use the amount called for in each recipe, it may be easier to dunk and thoroughly coat your food if you dole out a bit more egg substitute and Fiber One crumbs while preparing your dish.

✱ You can add almost any dry spice to the crumbs for extra flavor in your crunchy coating. Some HG staples are salt, black pepper, garlic powder, and onion powder. But feel free to experiment with cumin, cayenne pepper, nutmeg, lemon pepper seasoning, basil, and even taco seasoning mix (just not all at once!).

✱ Love to fiber-fry but hate having to break out the blender each and every time? Just whip up a super-sized batch of Fiber One crumbs and store 'em in an airtight container. FYI, ¼ cup of the crumbs is equal to ½ cup of the cereal.

✱ HG recipes featuring the Fiber One crumb coating generally taste best eaten hot out of the oven the day they're prepared. But if you wanna enjoy some leftovers the day after, do so by heating 'em briefly in the oven at a very high temperature. This way your crumb coating will stay crunchy!

spicy crispy chicken sandwich

PER SERVING (1 sandwich): 313 calories, 4.5g fat, 861mg sodium, 47g carbs, 12g fiber, 7g sugars, 31g protein

✳ Ingredients

3 ounces raw boneless skinless lean chicken breast
1 small hamburger bun (light, if available)
⅓ cup Fiber One bran cereal (original)
2 tablespoons fat-free mayonnaise
2 slices tomato
1 leaf romaine lettuce
¼ teaspoon cayenne pepper, divided
Dash of salt
Dash of black pepper
Dash of chili powder

✳ Directions

Preheat oven to 375 degrees.

Using a blender or food processor, grind Fiber One to a breadcrumb-like consistency. Add half of the cayenne pepper (⅛ teaspoon) to the crumbs and mix well. Place crumbs in one small dish and egg substitute in another.

Sprinkle salt and black pepper evenly on both sides of the chicken. Then coat chicken on both sides—first with egg substitute and then with seasoned crumbs.

Place chicken on a baking pan sprayed with nonstick spray. Top chicken with a light mist of nonstick spray and then place in oven. Cook for 10 minutes.

Flip the chicken over and add another light mist of nonstick spray. Cook for an additional 10 to 12 minutes, until chicken is fully cooked and coating looks crispy.

While the chicken is cooking, combine mayo, the remaining cayenne pepper, and the chili powder in a small bowl. Spread half of the mayo mixture on each half of the bun.

On the bun bottom, place chicken, tomato, and lettuce, and then top with the other half of the bun.

MAKES 1 SERVING

• •

Would You Rather . . .

So you decide to do some late-night snacking . . . Well, that half-pint of chocolate chip cookie dough ice cream likely contains at least 540 calories and 30 grams of fat. To work those calories off, you'd have to:

✱ Vacuum vigorously for about 2 hours (without breaks!) *or*

✱ Hand wash and dry dishes nonstop for well over 3 hours *or*

✱ Make and unmake the bed repeatedly for more than 4 hours straight!

Times based on estimates for a 150-pound woman.

7-layer burrito blitz

PER SERVING (1 burrito): 277 calories, 3g fat, 875mg sodium, 46g carbs, 14.5g fiber, 4g sugars, 22g protein

✳ Ingredients

1 medium low-fat flour tortilla (about 110 calories with at least 6g fiber)
⅓ cup canned black beans
1 ounce ground-beef-style soy crumbles
½ cup chopped iceberg lettuce
¼ cup chopped tomatoes
2 tablespoons chopped onions
2 tablespoons fat-free sour cream
2 tablespoons shredded fat-free cheese (Monterey Jack or cheddar)
Salt and black pepper, to taste

✳ Directions

Prepare crumbles according to package directions. Season crumbles to taste with salt and black pepper. Set aside.

Microwave tortilla until slightly warm. Layer ingredients in a long strip down the middle of the tortilla, starting with black beans and then adding crumbles, sour cream, lettuce, onions, cheese, and tomatoes.

Fold tortilla sides in first and then roll up from the bottom. Seven layers—all for you!

MAKES 1 SERVING

This is one super-stuffed burrito! You may want to revisit "Wrap It Up Right!", our tortilla tutorial on page 79, to freshen up on the basics of building the best burritos!

HG SHOCKER!

Think salads are a safe selection at the drive-thru? Guess again. Taco Bell's Fiesta Taco Salad, with 840 calories and 45 fat grams, is pretty much the worst thing on the menu! And just a serving of the honey mustard dressing *alone* at Burger King contains 270 calories and 23 grams of fat!

chapter six

manly meals

guy food rocks

it takes a real man to be a hungry girl.

Sometimes you just want a stick-to-your-ribs kinda meal. A Philly Cheesesteak, a big bowl of chili, a meaty pizza, or a chicken pot pie. If it's wimpy, diet-y food you're looking for, you're in the wrong place. Ready for food so good it'll fool your husbands, guy pals, boyfriends, and brothers? Here are HG's Manly Meals!

super-svelte bacon melt

✳ Ingredients

2 slices light bread (40 to 45 calories each with about 2g fiber per slice)
2 slices (about 1 ounce) extra-lean turkey bacon
2 slices fat-free American cheese
20 sprays I Can't Believe It's Not Butter! Spray

✳ Directions

Over medium heat, cook bacon strips in a pan sprayed with nonstick spray until crispy (about 5 minutes). Set aside.

Evenly spritz butter spray onto 1 side of each slice of bread, using 10 sprays per slice.

Top the unsprayed side of 1 slice of bread with a slice of cheese. Place bacon strips on top of cheese and cover with second slice of cheese. Next, top with the other bread slice (with the buttered side facing up).

Place sandwich in a heated pan sprayed with nonstick spray and cook over medium-low heat until bread is brown and toasty and cheese is nice and melty (1 to 2 minutes per side). Use a spatula to press down on the sandwich while it cooks.

Slice sandwich down the middle or diagonally, or just bite right into it!

MAKES 1 SERVING

cheesy chicken quesadilla

PER SERVING (1 quesadilla): 240 calories, 3g fat, 705mg sodium, 24g carbs, 9g fiber, 1g sugars, 34g protein

✶ Ingredients

1 medium low-fat flour tortilla (about 110 calories with at least 6g fiber)
2 ounces cooked boneless skinless lean chicken breast, sliced
⅓ cup shredded fat-free cheese (any flavor)
1 tablespoon diced scallions
Optional toppings: fat-free sour cream, salsa

✶ Directions

Over medium heat, set tortilla in a pan lightly spritzed with nonstick spray. Arrange the cheese evenly on top and then place chicken strips and scallions on half of the tortilla.

Once cheese begins to melt, fold the cheese-only side over the other side. (Use a spatula to press down firmly, securing the quesadilla's shape.) Continue to cook for a minute or so, flipping quesadilla halfway through.

Slide your quesadilla onto a plate and top with salsa and sour cream, if you like. Enjoy!

MAKES 1 SERVING

dan good chili

✶✶ *Dan's chili is insanely good and has become a staple at home and at the HG office. It's great alone, over Tofu Shirataki noodles, on a baked potato, as a side dish, or as a main meal. It definitely takes a lot longer to prepare than most HG recipes, but it is SO worth it! (BTW, not only is Dan the inventor of the world's best veggie chili, he's also my husband.)* ✶✶

✶ Ingredients

4 ¼ cups canned tomato sauce

1 cup canned diced tomatoes with green chilies

¾ cup canned black beans, drained and rinsed

¾ cup canned red kidney beans, drained and rinsed

½ cup canned jalapeño slices, chopped

1 cup canned sweet corn kernels, drained

1½ cups chopped onions

1 large red bell pepper, chopped

1 large green bell pepper, chopped

1¾ cups chopped carrots

1½ cups chopped portabello mushrooms

1½ tablespoons chili powder

2 teaspoons crushed garlic

1 teaspoon Worcestershire sauce

1 teaspoon ground cumin

Optional: salt

✳ Directions

Place the tomato sauce, tomatoes, jalapeños, chili powder, and cumin in a large pot. Stir over low heat. Once mixture is heated, stir in the garlic and continue to cook for about 5 minutes.

Add carrots and continue to cook over low heat. Meanwhile, over medium heat, cook onions, peppers, and mushrooms for 3 to 5 minutes in a large pan with just ½ cup of water (and some salt, if desired). The onions and peppers should still be a little crunchy. Using a slotted spoon to drain any excess water, add the veggies to the pot.

Add beans, corn, and Worcestershire sauce to the pot. Mix well. Everything should now be in the pot.

Cook over low heat for about 2 hours, stirring every 20 minutes or so. Chili is done when carrots have lost their crunch.

MAKES 10 SERVINGS

For Weight Watchers **POINTS**®
values and photos of all the
recipes in this book, check out
hungry-girl.com/book.

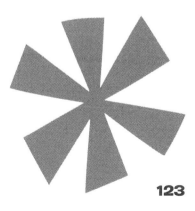

2-good twice-baked potato

✷ ✷ *This is one of the very first guilt-free recipe swaps I ever created. And to this day, it's still one of my favorites. I've fooled close to two hundred people over the years with these twice-baked potatoes. They're as creamy and delicious as any stuffed potato out there!* ✷ ✷

✶ Ingredients

1 medium (8-ounce) baking potato
1 slice fat-free American cheese
1 ounce fat-free liquid non-dairy creamer
Salt, paprika, and parsley, to taste

✶ Directions

Preheat oven to 375 degrees.

Puncture potato in several places with a fork. Peel the skin off the top of the potato and then cook potato in the microwave for 6 to 8 minutes.

Once potato is cool enough to handle, scoop out the insides, leaving behind an empty potato shell. Set shell aside.

Place potato pulp in a small dish and then add cheese, creamer, and a little salt. Mash it all together until the cheese melts, leaving a creamy, cheesy mashed potato mixture.

Place potato mixture back into the potato shell and sprinkle with paprika and parsley.

Place potato in a baking dish sprayed lightly with nonstick spray and bake in the oven for 20 to 30 minutes, until top is nice and brown.

MAKES 1 SERVING

• •

DUMP THESE CHUMPS!

Manly meals to avoid when you're out . . .

Spaghetti and meatballs (900 calories and 30g fat!)
Lasagna (870 calories and 50g fat!)
Pot Roast (730 calories and 35g fat!)
Fish and Chips (1,130 calories and 55g fat!)
Ribs (1,190 calories and 70g fat!)

Nutritional information based on averages.

"meaty" thin crust pizza

PER SERVING (1 pizza): 264 calories, 4.5g fat, 1,263mg sodium, 35g carbs, 12.5g fiber, 6g sugars, 27g protein

✶✶ *Feel free to season your sauce with any of your favorite spices. You can even add a little bit of Splenda for a sweet pizza sauce!* ✶✶

✶ Ingredients

1 medium low-fat flour tortilla (about 110 calories with at least 6g fiber)
1½ ounces ground-beef-style or sausage-style soy crumbles, thawed if previously frozen
⅓ cup shredded fat-free mozzarella cheese
⅓ cup canned tomato sauce
2 teaspoons reduced-fat Parmesan-style grated topping
¼ teaspoon garlic powder
Optional: salt, black pepper, oregano, onion powder, red pepper flakes, etc.

✶ Directions

Preheat oven to 375 degrees.

Place tortilla in a baking pan sprayed lightly with nonstick spray and bake in the oven for 5 to 6 minutes on each side, until slightly crispy.

Combine tomato sauce and garlic powder. Season sauce to taste with the optional ingredients, if desired. Remove tortilla from oven and spread on tomato sauce.

Next, sprinkle crumbles, cheese, and grated topping evenly over sauce. Return pizza to the oven for about 5 minutes or until cheese has melted and crumbles are hot.

If you like, top pizza with optional ingredients. Use a pizza cutter or a sharp knife to cut into slices.

MAKES 1 SERVING

HG Tip: Counting sodium? Save around 400mg by using no-salt-added tomato sauce.

t-rific turkey reuben

PER SERVING (1 sandwich): 282 calories, 7g fat, 1,448mg sodium, 35g carbs, 3.5g fiber, 6g sugars, 23g protein

✴ Ingredients

2 slices rye bread (reduced-calorie, if available)

2 ounces (about 4 slices) Oscar Mayer 98% fat free oven roasted turkey breast

¼ cup well-drained sauerkraut

1 slice reduced-fat Swiss cheese (4 grams of fat or fewer)

4 teaspoons fat-free Thousand Island dressing

20 sprays I Can't Believe It's Not Butter! Spray

✴ Directions

Evenly spritz butter spray on 1 side of each slice of bread, using 10 sprays per slice. Spread non-buttered sides evenly with the dressing.

With the buttered side down, top one slice with sauerkraut, cheese, and turkey. Then top with the remaining slice of bread, buttered-side up.

Cook sandwich in a pan sprayed with nonstick spray over medium-low heat, occasionally pressing down on sandwich with a spatula. Flipping once or twice, grill until both sides are browned and crisp. Serve immediately.

MAKES 1 SERVING

HG Tip: Watching your salt intake? Cook up your own turkey breast and save about 500mg of sodium. Packaged deli meats are super-high in the stuff!

kickin' chicken pot pie

PER SERVING (¼th of pie): 235 calories, 6g fat, 723mg sodium, 26g carbs, 3.5g fiber, 6g sugars, 18g protein

✴✴ *This chicken pot pie is a surprisingly authentic swap for the real thing. The reduced-fat crescent topping is the best part. Yum!* ✴✴

✴ Ingredients

8 ounces raw boneless skinless lean chicken breast, cut into bite-sized pieces

3 cups frozen mixed vegetables

One 10.75-ounce can Campbell's 98% Fat Free Cream of Celery Soup

3 servings Pillsbury Reduced Fat Crescent Rolls refrigerated dough

✴ Directions

Preheat oven to 350 degrees.

Cook chicken pieces for several minutes in a pan spritzed with nonstick spray, until chicken is light brown (cooked but still tender). Set aside.

Heat frozen veggies in the microwave according to package instructions.

Mix chicken, vegetables, and soup together, and then place in a 9-inch round baking dish sprayed with nonstick spray. Place dish in the oven and bake for about 30 minutes or until mixture is hot and bubbly, stirring halfway through.

While dish is cooking, unroll 3 crescent rolls. Use your hands to combine pieces into one large ball of dough. With a rolling pin, roll dough out (super-thin) into a circle just large enough to fit inside the dish (a little less than 9 inches wide).

Add dough to the top of the mixture and cook for an additional 15 to 20 minutes, until top is golden brown.

MAKES 4 SERVINGS

Dig hearty meat-packed pies? Check out the Squash-tastic Shepherd's Pie on page 278 in the butternut squash section of the "Fun With . . ." chapter!

• •

Would You Rather . . .

It doesn't get any manlier than inhaling an entire chicken pot pie. But if you decide to eat the real deal (instead of HG's slimmed-down swap), it can *easily* cost you 850 calories and 50 plus grams of fat! To burn that off, you'd have to:

* ✳ Spend 2 whole hours shoveling your way out of a snowstorm *or*
* ✳ Manually mow the lawn for more than 2 hours straight *or*
* ✳ Rake leaves vigorously for about 3 hours!

Times based on estimates for a 150-pound woman.

sloppy janes

✳✳ *Heads Up! These Sloppy Janes are a little sweet because, well, that's the way I like 'em! If you don't like yours sweet, feel free to leave out the Splenda.* ✳✳

✳ Ingredients

1 pound raw extra-lean ground turkey

5 small hamburger buns (light, if available)

½ cup chopped onions

½ cup chopped red bell peppers

1 cup canned tomato sauce

¾ cup canned no-salt-added tomato sauce

2 tablespoons tomato paste

1½ tablespoons Splenda No Calorie Sweetener (granulated)

1 tablespoon red wine vinegar

1 tablespoon Worcestershire sauce

1 teaspoon steak seasoning blend, dry

Dash of salt

✳ Directions

Spray a large pan with nonstick spray and bring to medium-high heat. Add turkey to the pan. Spread the meat around in the pan to break it up a bit.

In a small dish, combine Splenda, salt, and steak seasoning. Sprinkle this mixture over the meat and continue to stir meat in the pan. Once the meat has browned, reduce heat to medium.

Add onions, peppers, Worcestershire sauce, and vinegar to the pan. Stir and then continue to cook for 5 minutes.

Add tomato sauces and tomato paste to the pan and stir well. Reduce heat to low and cook the mixture for an additional 5 minutes.

Toast the buns, if desired. Put one-fifth of the mixture on each bottom bun and then finish off with tops of the buns.

MAKES 5 SERVINGS

CHEW ON THIS:

More than half a billion pounds of bacon are produced in the U.S. each year. You don't want to know how many calories and fat grams that adds up to!

crazy-good turkey taco meatloaf

PER SERVING (⅙th of loaf): 127 calories, 1g fat, 688mg sodium, 7g carbs, 0.5g fiber, 2g sugars, 22g protein

✷✷ This turkey taco meatloaf is addictive! Once you start eating it, it's hard to stop. Luckily, it's super-low in calories and packed with good-for-you stuff. ✷✷

✷ Ingredients

1 pound raw extra-lean ground turkey
2 slices fat-free cheddar cheese
½ cup shredded fat-free cheddar cheese
½ cup canned sweet corn kernels
¼ cup chopped green bell peppers
¼ cup chopped onions
½ cup salsa
½ packet of taco seasoning mix, dry

✷ Directions

Preheat oven to 375 degrees.

Cook peppers and onions for 3 minutes over medium heat in a pan sprayed with nonstick spray.

In a large bowl, combine onions and peppers with turkey, corn, and seasoning mix. Spread half of the mixture evenly into the bottom of a loaf pan (about 9" x 5") sprayed with nonstick spray.

Layer the two slices of fat-free cheese on top of the mixture (try to keep slices away from the pan's edges). Evenly top with the remaining meat mixture.

Pour the salsa over the top of the loaf. Cook in the oven for 30 minutes.

Top loaf with shredded cheese. Return loaf to the oven and cook for another 15 minutes.

MAKES 6 SERVINGS

CHEW ON THIS:

Meatloaf recipes first appeared in American cookbooks in the 1880s!

meat-lovers' cheesy pasta

PER SERVING (entire recipe): 301 calories, 3.5g fat,
1,277mg sodium, 20g carbs, 7.5g fiber, 6g sugars, 49g protein

✳ Ingredients

1 package House Foods Tofu Shirataki, Spaghetti Shape
3 ounces cooked boneless skinless lean chicken breast,
    cut into bite-sized pieces
1½ ounces ground-beef-style soy crumbles, thawed if
    previously frozen
⅓ cup shredded fat-free cheddar cheese
½ cup canned tomato sauce
⅛ teaspoon garlic powder
Salt and black pepper, to taste

*Never worked
with Tofu Shirataki
before? Turn to
page 261 for
helpful hints!*

✳ Directions

Rinse and drain noodles well.
Pat dry. Place noodles in a
microwave-safe bowl and microwave
for 1 minute.

Drain excess liquid from noodles and
pat them until thoroughly dry. Cut
noodles into spaghetti-length pieces. Set aside.

Heat chicken and soy crumbles, either in a pan sprayed with nonstick spray or
in the microwave.

Combine noodles, chicken, crumbles, cheese, tomato sauce, and garlic powder, and mix well.

Microwave entire dish for 1 additional minute. Season to taste with salt and black pepper. Enjoy your feast!

MAKES 1 SERVING

> **HG Tip:** Sodium counters can save about 600mg of the stuff by using no-salt-added tomato sauce— justremember to season it up!

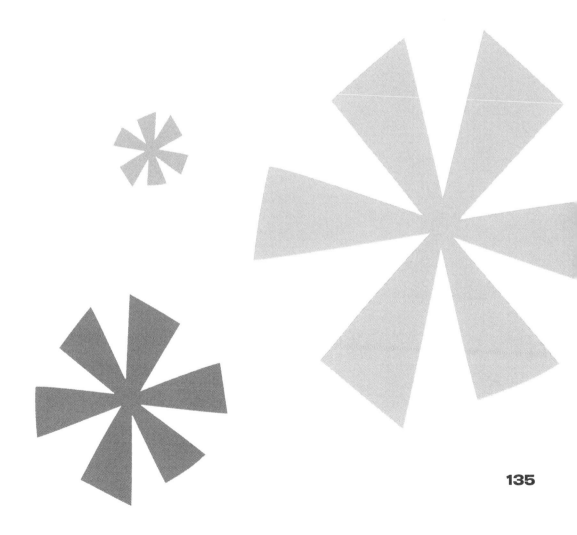

phenomenal philly cheesesteak

PER SERVING (1 sandwich): 301 calories, 9g fat, 588mg sodium, 28g carbs, 0.5g fiber, 7g sugars, 26g protein

✳✳ *This Philly Cheesesteak is as good as (if not better than!) any you'd find ANYWHERE (including Philadelphia).* ✳✳

✳ Ingredients

3 ounces raw lean filet beefsteak
1 hot dog bun
1 slice fat-free American cheese
⅓ cup sliced onions

✳ Directions

Slice your filet into thin strips. (Freezing it slightly beforehand will make it easier to cut.)

Cook onions over medium-high heat in a pan spritzed with nonstick spray for about 5 minutes, until onion slices are slightly browned. Remove onions from the pan and set aside.

Spritz a little more nonstick spray into the pan (remove pan from heat before re-spraying) and cook filet strips over medium-high heat for 1 to 2 minutes, flipping them halfway through cooking.

Place cheese on top of meat (still in the pan) and continue to cook until cheese is slightly melted.

Meanwhile, warm or toast your bun. Place meat and cheese in the bun and then top with onions. Enjoy.

MAKES 1 SERVING

* *

STEAK 101—Tips 'n Tricks!
All steaks are NOT created equal. Know your beef . . .

* Leaner cuts include filet mignon and sirloin.

* Fattier, marbled cuts include shell steak and rib eye. These often contain more calories than leaner steak cuts.

* Your best bet is often the filet mignon. Not only is it leaner but it's also often served in smaller portions than other cuts.

* A porterhouse steak usually weighs in at about 20 ounces, and it's actually two steaks in one (a filet and a strip). A 20-ounce porterhouse steak has about 1,400 calories and 100 grams of fat. Yikes!

baja taco blitz

PER SERVING (2 tacos): 347 calories, 6.5g fat, 380mg sodium,
36g carbs, 6.5g fiber, 5g sugars, 36g protein

This recipe was co-developed with Weight Watchers®.

✶✶ *Are you a taco-lover? You'll FREAK over these!!!* ✶✶

✶ Ingredients

2 small corn tortillas
4 ounces raw boneless skinless lean chicken breast, cut into strips
½ small onion, sliced
¼ large red bell pepper, sliced
⅛ avocado (2 small slices)
½ cup chopped iceberg lettuce
2 tablespoons shredded fat-free cheese
  (cheddar or Monterey Jack)
2 tablespoons fat-free sour cream
1 tablespoon salsa
1 teaspoon chopped cilantro
Salt and black pepper, to taste

✶ Directions

Spray a pan with nonstick spray and set stove to medium heat. Cook onion slices
in the pan for 2 minutes.

Add pepper slices to the pan and continue to cook for an additional 2 minutes until veggies are a little crisp. Remove veggies from the pan and place them in a bowl.

Cook chicken strips in the pan until cooked throughout and then add them to the bowl with the onions and peppers.

Heat tortillas in the pan for 20 seconds on each side. Remove and plate tortillas.

Season the onions, peppers, and chicken to taste with salt and black pepper, and then place them evenly into the center of each tortilla.

Place one slice of avocado on each tortilla. Finish by topping with lettuce, cheese, sour cream, salsa, and cilantro. Roll 'em up and enjoy!

MAKES 1 SERVING

 For a pic of this recipe, see the photo insert. Yay!

chapter seven

party time

party & holiday foods
it's my party and I'll chew if I want to.

Some people believe that you should *never* serve guilt-free foods at parties, family gatherings, or holiday get-togethers. Those people have clearly *not* been exposed to the recipes in this chapter. These are so good that no one will *ever* know they're not LOADED with tons of fat and calories. There's nothing fake-tasting or diet-y about any of these crowd-pleasers. Promise!

hg's de-pudged pigs in a blanket

PER SERVING (4 pigs in a blanket): 134 calories, 5g fat, 652mg sodium, 16g carbs, 0g fiber, 3g sugars, 8g protein

✳ Ingredients

8 fat-free or nearly fat-free hot dogs (40 to 50 calories each)
1 can (8 servings) Pillsbury Reduced Fat Crescent Rolls refrigerated dough

✳ Directions

Preheat oven to 375 degrees.

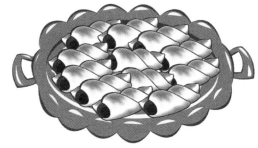

Cut each hot dog into 4 even pieces.

Take 1 of the 8 triangle-shaped portions of the dough and stretch or roll it out slightly, making it into a larger triangle. Then cut this piece of dough into 4 long, narrow triangles. Beginning at the base of each of these triangles, roll 1 hot dog piece up in each triangle until the point of the triangle wraps around the center. Place your blanketed pigs on a large, ungreased baking pan and repeat entire process 7 more times with remaining dough and hot dog pieces. (Be sure to evenly space them, as the dough will expand while baking.)

Place pan in the oven and cook for about 12 minutes, until dough appears slightly browned and crispy. Enjoy!

MAKES 8 SERVINGS

 For a pic of this recipe, see the photo insert. Yay!

merry marinated veggies

PER SERVING (1 cup): 58 calories, 1g fat, 22mg sodium, 11g carbs, 1.5g fiber, 10g sugars, 1g protein

✳✳ *These veggies taste even better the second day!* ✳✳

✳ Ingredients

1 large cucumber, thinly sliced
1 medium red bell pepper, thinly sliced
1 medium zucchini, halved lengthwise and cut into ½-inch-wide strips
1 cup thinly sliced red onions
1 cup balsamic vinegar
1 teaspoon olive oil
4 no-calorie sweetener packets
Salt and black pepper, to taste

✳ Directions

Combine vinegar, oil, and sweetener with 1 cup of water.

Place all veggies in a separate dish. Cover veggies with vinegar marinade and stir. Cover dish and refrigerate for at least 1 day.

Season to taste with salt and black pepper.

MAKES 5 SERVINGS

For Weight Watchers *POINTS*® values and photos of all the recipes in this book, check out hungry-girl.com/book.

snack-tastic holiday mix

✳✳ *This stuff is so good, it's gonna take a lot of restraint to not down it all in one sitting. So invite some friends over ASAP to share it with you!* ✳✳

✳ Ingredients

2 cups puffed corn cereal (like Kix)

½ cup Fiber One bran cereal (original)

1 ounce (about 1 cup) crispy freeze-dried apples

3 tablespoons Splenda No Calorie Sweetener (granulated)

1½ tablespoons light whipped butter or
light buttery spread

1 tablespoon light corn syrup

½ teaspoon cinnamon

1 tablespoon sliced almonds

✳ Directions

Since this is a quickie recipe, it's best to have all ingredients measured out and ready to go before starting, in order to avoid burning. Begin by setting out a large piece of foil for the recipe to cool on after it's prepared.

In a medium saucepan, combine butter, Splenda, corn syrup, and cinnamon. Stir while cooking over low heat. Once mixture is thoroughly blended and bubbling, stir in both cereals and coat them with the mixture. Continuously stir for about 2½ minutes, until cereal mix looks well coated and toasty.

Mix in apple crisps and almonds, and then immediately remove from heat. Spread mixture out on foil until cool.

MAKES 4 SERVINGS

• •

HG HOLIDAY SHOCKER!
A slice of that pecan pie sounds delicious, but it likely has at least 600 calories and more than 30 grams of fat. That pie is packing more than just pecans!

jalapeño swappers

✶✶ *These poppers are so good, your guests will* never *know they're low in fat and calories! But remember to remove* all *the seeds—they're super-spicy!* ✶✶

✶ Ingredients

5 fresh whole jalapeños
½ cup Fiber One bran cereal (original)
¼ cup fat-free liquid egg substitute
¼ cup fat-free cream cheese
¼ cup shredded fat-free cheddar cheese
Optional: salt, black pepper, garlic powder

For the 411 on faux-frying with Fiber One, see page 113!

✶ Directions

Preheat oven to 350 degrees.

Halve the jalapeños lengthwise and remove the seeds, stems, and membranes. Be *very* careful when handling jalapeños. Wash your hands frequently and well, and avoid touching your face and eyes. Wash halves and dry them very well. Set aside.

Stir together cream cheese and shredded cheese. If you like, season cheese mixture with salt, black pepper, and/or garlic powder.

Using a blender or food processor, grind Fiber One to a breadcrumb-like consistency. If you like, season crumbs with salt, black pepper, and/or garlic powder. Place crumbs in one small dish and egg substitute in another.

Stuff each jalapeño half with the cheese mixture. Next, carefully coat both sides of each jalapeño half, first with egg substitute and then with Fiber One crumbs.

Place jalapeños on a baking pan sprayed with nonstick spray and place in the oven. Cook for 25 minutes (for very spicy poppers) to 30 minutes (medium-hot poppers).

MAKES 2 SERVINGS

• •

100 Calories—This or That?

Looking for a 100-calorie party food? Would you rather have . . .

6 chilled shrimp dipped in cocktail sauce *or*
1 breaded, fried shrimp with sweet and sour sauce?

3 whole cups of popcorn *or*
2 tablespoons of mixed nuts?

1 full skewer of grilled chicken *or*
1 tiny triangle of a chicken quesadilla?

10 baked tortilla chips with a side of salsa *or*
1 loaded nacho?

A plate full of crisp veggies with some spinach dip *or*
1 mini spinach quiche?

Nutritional information based on averages.

save-the-day stuffing

PER SERVING (1 cup): 89 calories, 1.5g fat, 275mg sodium, 17g carbs, 4g fiber, 4g sugars, 5g protein

✳ Ingredients

6 slices light bread (40 to 45 calories each with about 2g fiber per slice)
1 cup chopped onions
1 cup chopped celery
1 cup chopped mushrooms
1 cup fat-free broth (chicken or vegetable), at room temperature
¼ cup fat-free liquid egg substitute
1 tablespoon light whipped butter or light buttery spread
2 teaspoons minced garlic
Salt, black pepper, rosemary, and thyme, to taste

✳ Directions

For best results, leave bread uncovered for a night or two, until slightly stale. Otherwise, begin by lightly toasting bread.

Preheat oven to 350 degrees.

Cut bread into ½-inch cubes. Spray a medium baking dish with nonstick spray and place bread cubes evenly along the bottom of the dish.

In a medium pot, combine broth, celery, and onions. Cook for 8 minutes over medium heat.

Remove pot from heat and add mushrooms and garlic. Season mixture to taste with salt, black pepper, rosemary, and thyme. Let cool for several minutes.

Add egg substitute and butter to veggie/broth mixture and stir. Pour mixture into the baking pan, evenly covering bread cubes. Mix gently with a fork. Bread cubes should be moist, but not saturated. If necessary, add 1 to 2 tablespoons of water and then mix again.

Cover with foil and cook dish in the oven for 20 minutes.

Remove foil and fluff and rearrange stuffing. Return dish to oven, uncovered, and cook for an additional 15 minutes.

MAKES 5 SERVINGS

HG Tip: *Zazzle up your stuffing by adding any of the following to it before baking: 1 ounce of raisins, 1 medium pear (chopped), 2 tablespoons of sliced almonds, 1 ounce of sweetened dried cranberries, or 1 medium Granny Smith apple (chopped). Each one adds less than 20 calories to each serving!*

party poppin' trail mix

PER SERVING (1 generous cup): 118 calories, 3.5g fat, 83mg sodium, 22g carbs, 5g fiber, 9g sugars, 4g protein

✶ Ingredients

2 cups popped 94% fat-free kettle corn microwave popcorn

1 cup puffed corn cereal (like Kix)

½ cup Fiber One bran cereal (original)

2 ounces chocolate-covered soy nuts

1 ounce (about 1 cup) freeze-dried fruit

✶ Directions

Combine all ingredients and give 'em a shake. Wasn't that easy?

MAKES 5 SERVINGS

**dreamy chocolate
peanut butter fudge p. 171**

breakfast

tutti frutti crunch yogurt parfait p. 22

eggs bene-chick p. 2

bring on the breakfast pizza p. 18

yummy butternut home fries p. 280

junk food

g bopper burger stopper w/cheese p. 106

loaded 'n oated veggie pizza p. 92

lord of the onion rings p. 104

cookie-rific ice cream freeze p. 239

lunches & mini meals

hacked 'n whacked santa fe shrimp supreme p. 34

noodled-up zucchini pancakes p. 2

squash-tastic shepherd's pie p. 278

so-good turkey club wrap p. 78

baja taco blitz p. 138

my big fat greek pita p. 70

crazy-good cold sesame noodles p. 264

cocktails & party fun

piña colada freeze p. 2◄

amazing ate-layer dip p. 158

i can't believe it's not sweet potato pie p. 164

ey-gooey chili cheese nachos p. 99

hg's de-pudged pigs in a blanket p. 142

magical low-calorie margarita p. 244

rockin' restaurant spinach dip p. 154

sweet stuff

chocolate pudding crunch explosion p. 182

layered berry custard crostata p. 1

caramel pumpkin pudding cupcakes p. 212

pb 'n chocolate bread pudding bonanza p. 174

cheesy dog tortilla roll-ups

PER SERVING (2 pieces): 78 calories, 1g fat, 476mg sodium, 10g carbs, 3g fiber, 1g sugars, 9g protein

✷ ✷ *These are awesome (and easy-to-make) mini hors d'oeuvres!* ✷ ✷

✷ Ingredients

2 fat-free or nearly fat-free hot dogs (40 to 50 calories each)
1 medium low-fat flour tortilla (about 110 calories with at least 6g fiber)
¼ cup shredded fat-free cheese (cheddar or American)

✷ Directions

Microwave hot dogs according to directions on package.

Slice tortilla in half. Sprinkle cheese evenly on top of both halves, avoiding the edges. Heat tortilla halves in the microwave for about 20 seconds, until cheese is just slightly melted.

Immediately roll 1 hot dog in each cheesed-up tortilla half by placing the dog at the straight side of the tortilla and then rolling it up tightly.

Toast roll-ups in the toaster oven until desired crispiness is reached. Slice each roll-up into thirds, and then serve with toothpicks.

MAKES 3 SERVINGS

rockin' lean bean casserole

PER SERVING (1/10th of casserole): 76 calories, 2g fat,
431mg sodium, 13g carbs, 3.5g fiber, 4g sugars, 3g protein

✶ ✶ *This recipe will rock your holiday world! The key here is to find really awesome onion-flavored soy crisps.* ✶ ✶

✶ Ingredients

Two 16-ounce bags frozen French-style green beans, thawed, drained,
and thoroughly dried
Two 10.75-ounce cans Campbell's 98% Fat Free Cream of Celery Soup
One 8-ounce can sliced water chestnuts, drained
1 ounce (about 25 pieces) onion-flavored soy crisps, crushed

✶ Directions

Preheat oven to 325 degrees.

Make sure green beans are thoroughly drained and completely dry—use a towel if you need to. Then place half of the green beans in a casserole dish (a 2- to 3-quart rectangular one works best).

Pour 1 can of the soup evenly on top of the layer of green beans. Place half of the sliced water chestnuts over the soup layer.

Cover with remaining green beans and then top with the rest of the soup. Evenly top with the remaining water chestnuts. Place dish in the oven and cook for 45 minutes.

Top with crushed soy crisps and return dish to the oven for another 10 minutes or so, until crisps turn golden brown.

MAKES 10 SERVINGS

• •

TOP ATE Party Survival Tips
Hungry Girl's guide to food-happy festivities . . .

1. Never show up super-hungry. Eat something light before you head to the party.

2. Wear fitted party clothes. Doing so will help keep you from shamelessly stuffing too much food down your gullet!

3. Drink 1 to 2 glasses of water right before or right after you arrive at the party. This will help you feel fuller and curb cravings.

4. Don't eat anything during your first 20 to 30 minutes at the party. Mingle, socialize, and don't stand on top of the food.

5. Don't get caught empty-handed. Always have a drink in one hand (stick to no-cal beverages for most of the night!) and maybe a little clutch purse in the other. This way you'll be less likely to graze, because your hands will be full.

6. Don't deprive yourself. It's okay to enjoy some treats, just remember to do so in moderation.

7. Make a deal with yourself. Only after eating 5 pieces of something "good" (like veggies from the veggie tray), allow yourself to indulge in one piece of something "bad" (like cookies or candy). You'll likely fill up before you even hit round 2 of the bad stuff!

8. Watch what you drink. Eggnog, spiced cider, and hot cocoa can all be diet-busting disasters and a complete waste of calories. You are better off reaching for water or other no-calorie drinks.

rockin' restaurant spinach dip

PER SERVING (3 heaping tablespoons): 72 calories, 1g fat,
310mg sodium, 9g carbs, 1g fiber, 4g sugars, 7g protein

✳︎✳︎ *This dip is so good, it may actually bring tears to your eyes. It's great with pita chips, mixed into egg whites, or stirred into Tofu Shirataki noodles!* ✳︎✳︎

✳ Ingredients

One 10-ounce package frozen chopped spinach, thawed and drained thoroughly
4 ounces canned sliced water chestnuts, chopped
4 ounces fat-free block cheese (any kind)
3 tablespoons plus 1 teaspoon reduced-fat Parmesan-style grated topping
⅓ cup plus 2 teaspoons fat-free mayonnaise
¼ cup fat-free sour cream
1 ounce light soymilk
2 tablespoons minced shallots
1 teaspoon minced garlic
Salt and black pepper, to taste

✳ Directions

Preheat oven to 325 degrees.

Cook garlic and shallots over
medium heat in a pan sprayed with
nonstick spray, until softened but not burned (a minute or two). Set aside.

In a medium saucepan, melt block cheese over a low flame with the soymilk,
stirring occasionally.

Once cheese has melted and the mixture is well blended, add mayo, sour cream, and Parmesan. Stir until thoroughly mixed (still over low heat).

Next, add garlic, shallots, and water chestnuts and stir. Add spinach to the pot and mix thoroughly.

Spoon dip into a medium casserole dish and bake in the oven for 20 to 25 minutes.

Voilà! Your spinach-y masterpiece is complete. Season to taste with salt and black pepper.

MAKES 8 SERVINGS

 For a pic of this recipe, see the photo insert. Yay!

· ·

HG HOLIDAY SHOCKER!
What's a party without chips and dip? While that onion dip might seem like a good choice, be aware that just 2 measly little tablespoons contain about 60 calories and 6 grams of fat. That's only about 2 chips' worth!

no-nonsense nog

PER SERVING (1 cup): 98 calories, 2g fat, 382mg sodium, 13g carbs, 0.5g fiber, 6g sugars, 6g protein

✳ Ingredients

5 cups light vanilla soymilk
1 small (4-serving) package sugar-free fat-free vanilla instant pudding mix
6 no-calorie sweetener packets
1 teaspoon imitation rum extract
½ teaspoon nutmeg

✳ Directions

Combine all ingredients in a blender and blend on high until mixed thoroughly. Refrigerate for a few hours to allow nog to thicken.

MAKES 5 SERVINGS

HG HOLIDAY SHOCKER!
A cup of eggnog usually clocks in with more than 400 calories and 20 grams of fat. Eeek!

guilt-free dirt & worms surprise

PER SERVING (⅔ cup): 159 calories, 1g fat, 403mg sodium, 30g carbs, 1g fiber, 15g sugars, 7g protein

✷✷ *This is the perfect recipe for Halloween or kids' birthday parties.* ✷✷

✷ Ingredients

2 small (4-serving) packages sugar-free fat-free instant chocolate pudding mix
4 cups fat-free milk
4 sheets (16 crackers) chocolate graham crackers, crushed
12 gummy worms, chopped into thirds

✷ Directions

To make the pudding, add both packages of pudding mix to the milk and beat with a whisk for 2 to 4 minutes, until pudding is thoroughly mixed and thickened.

Pour pudding into a wide serving bowl. Place in the fridge for at least 15 minutes to set.

Once ready to serve, top pudding with worms. Then evenly distribute crushed graham crackers on top of worms.

MAKES 8 SERVINGS

For Weight Watchers *POINTS*® values and photos of all the recipes in this book, check out hungry-girl.com/book.

amazing ate-layer dip

PER SERVING (about 1 cup): 105 calories, 0.5g fat,
323mg sodium, 19g carbs, 4g fiber, 3g sugars, 7g protein

✳ ✳ *This dish is delicious served hot or cold. The seasoned butternut squash layer is the perfect swap for refried beans!* ✳ ✳

✳ Ingredients

4 cups shredded iceberg lettuce

2½ cups peeled and cubed butternut squash

2 cups cherry tomatoes, chopped

1 cup diced onions

1 cup canned black beans, heated (if desired)

4 ounces ground-beef-style soy crumbles, thawed if previously frozen

4 ounces roasted red peppers (not packed in oil), chopped

½ cup fat-free sour cream

¼ cup shredded fat-free cheddar cheese

3½ teaspoons taco seasoning mix, dry

Optional: salt, black pepper, lime juice

For the 411 on getting perfectly cubed squash, take a peek at "Butternut Squash Basics" on page 279!

✳ Directions

Combine half of the tomatoes with all of the onions. Season to taste with salt, black pepper, and lime juice, if desired. Set aside.

Next, nuke squash in a covered microwave-safe dish with 2 tablespoons of water for 6 to 7 minutes, until squash is tender enough to mash.

Using a fork or potato masher, mash squash to a pulp. Mix in 1 ½ teaspoons of the taco seasoning and set dish aside.

Combine soy crumbles with the remaining tomatoes, and 2 teaspoons of taco seasoning, in a heated pan sprayed with nonstick spray. Cook over a medium flame, stirring occasionally, until heated and mixed.

In a large dish, layer ingredients in this order: lettuce, butternut squash mixture, tomato/onion mix, sour cream, black beans, "meat" mixture, shredded cheese, red peppers.

MAKES 8 SERVINGS

 For a pic of this recipe, see the photo insert. Yay!

. . . .

Would You Rather . . .

The family holiday party is here. At the cocktail hour, you chow down on six hors d'oeuvres (adding up to about 350 calories and 25 grams of fat!). And that's *before* one bite of your dinner! Just to burn off the calories in those hors d'oeuvres, you would have to:

❋ Dance embarrassingly fast with your cousin for a little more than an hour *or*

❋ Clean up post-party for 1½ hours (with no company or help . . . sad!) *or*

❋ Wrap and rewrap Aunt Margie's gifts (she likes them perfect) for almost 5 hours!

Times based on estimates for a 150-pound woman.

portabello skinny "skins"

PER SERVING (1 mushroom): 67 calories, 0.5g fat,
404mg sodium, 6g carbs, 1.5g fiber, 2g sugars, 10g protein

✳✳ *This recipe was inspired by HG's pals over at the Mushroom Council. It makes an awesome party starter if you cut the "skins" into wedges and then serve them with toothpicks.* ✳✳

✳ Ingredients

4 large portabello mushroom caps
2 slices (about 1 ounce) extra-lean turkey bacon
⅔ cup shredded fat-free cheddar cheese
1 small tomato, chopped
1 tablespoon minced scallions
¼ teaspoon salt
⅛ teaspoon black pepper

✳ Directions

Preheat oven to 450 degrees.

Over medium heat, cook bacon strips, in a pan sprayed with nonstick spray, until crispy (about 5 minutes). Once cool enough to handle, crumble bacon into small pieces and set aside.

Line a baking pan with foil and spray lightly with nonstick spray. Wipe mushrooms clean with a moist paper towel and then let them dry.

Spritz caps lightly with nonstick spray (mist both sides as well as mushroom edges). Sprinkle the flat side with salt and black pepper, and then place, rounded-side down, on the baking pan.

Divide cheese among mushroom caps. Bake for 10 minutes in the oven or until cheese melts and edges begin to brown.

Remove pan from oven and sprinkle bacon, tomato, and scallions over mushrooms.

Return pan to oven and cook for an additional 5 minutes or until mushrooms are thoroughly heated.

MAKES 4 SERVINGS

HG HOLIDAY SHOCKER!

Stuffed mushrooms may seem like a great option (they are vegetables, right?!), but just 6 small stuffed mushrooms at your average party can contain as much as 400 calories and 30 grams of fat! Yuck!

crazy-creamy
crab-stuffed mushrooms

✳ Ingredients

12 medium (about 2 inches wide) brown mushroom caps

2 ounces drained white crabmeat

2 tablespoons minced celery

2 tablespoons minced red bell peppers

1 wedge The Laughing Cow Light Original Swiss cheese

1 tablespoon fat-free sour cream

1 tablespoon fat-free cream cheese

2 teaspoons fat-free cheese-flavored sprinkles

✳ Directions

Preheat oven to 375 degrees.

Wipe mushrooms clean with a damp paper towel and then dry them with a dry paper towel. Place, rounded-side down, on a baking dish sprayed lightly with nonstick spray.

In a small dish, thoroughly combine all other ingredients. Evenly spoon crab mixture into the mushroom caps.

Place baking dish in the oven for 10 to 12 minutes, until mushrooms are hot. Enjoy the creamy, crab-tastic goodness!

MAKES 3 SERVINGS

yummy yummy eggplant goo

PER SERVING (¼ cup): 37 calories, 1g fat, 295mg sodium, 7g carbs, 2.5g fiber, 3g sugars, 1g protein

✶ ✶ *This veggie-packed dip is a party must! It's great with warm pita pieces or cut-up veggies. But don't be surprised if you find some guests hovering over the bowl eating it straight. I keep this dish in the fridge and eat it in egg scrambles, on salads and sandwiches, and as a side dish. YUM!!! (Pssst . . . it's not really a goo—I just liked the name!)* ✶ ✶

✶ Ingredients

1 medium eggplant, peeled and cut into 1-inch cubes
1 medium red onion, chopped
½ red bell pepper, chopped
½ yellow bell pepper, chopped
¼ cup halved cherry tomatoes
1 tablespoon chopped garlic
1 tablespoon tomato paste
½ tablespoon olive oil
1 teaspoon salt
¼ teaspoon black pepper

✶ Directions

Preheat oven to 400 degrees.

Arrange all vegetables in a baking pan sprayed with nonstick spray. Sprinkle with garlic, olive oil, salt, and black pepper. Toss well.

Place pan in the oven and roast for about 40 minutes (until vegetables are tender), mixing occasionally.

Once cool enough to handle, place the contents of the pan into a blender with the tomato paste. Pulse several times until dip is chunky. (Do not process until smooth.)

MAKES 8 SERVINGS

i can't believe it's not sweet potato pie

PER SERVING (¼th of pie): 113 calories, <0.5g fat, 263mg sodium, 26g carbs, 1.5g fiber, 8g sugars, 5g protein

✶✶ *You may want to make a double batch of this stuff. It always goes fast at parties!* ✶✶

✶ Ingredients

1 large butternut squash (large enough to yield 2 cups mashed flesh)
½ cup fat-free liquid egg substitute
⅓ cup light vanilla soymilk
⅓ cup sugar-free maple syrup
¼ cup Splenda No Calorie Sweetener (granulated)
1 teaspoon cinnamon
½ teaspoon vanilla extract
¼ teaspoon salt
⅔ cup miniature marshmallows

✶ Directions

Preheat oven to 350 degrees.

Use a sharp knife to remove both ends of the squash. Peel squash and cut into large chunks, removing seeds.

Fill a large, microwave-safe dish with ½ inch of water. Place squash into the dish and cover. Microwave for about 8 minutes and then drain (squash should be tender enough to mash, but not overcooked).

With a potato masher, food processor, or fork, mash squash thoroughly. Measure out 2 generous cups, lightly packed, and place in a baking dish.

Add all ingredients except for the marshmallows to the dish. Mix ingredients thoroughly, but do not over-stir (squash should still be pulpy). Bake in the oven for 45 to 50 minutes, until solid and not liquidy.

Top the "pie" with mini marshmallows. Return to the oven for 5 minutes or until marshmallows begin to brown. Allow to cool before serving.

MAKES 4 SERVINGS

> *For b-nut squash cooking tips (and more squash-tastic recipes), visit the butternut squash section of the "Fun With . . ." chapter on page 276!*

 For a pic of this recipe, see the photo insert. Yay!

· ·

HG HOLIDAY SHOCKER!
Sweet potato pie often has about 350 calories and 16 grams of fat per slice. And remember, it's just a SIDE DISH.

sassy veggie egg rolls

PER SERVING (2 pieces): 82 calories, <0.5g fat, 285mg sodium, 18g carbs, 1.5g fiber, 3g sugars, 3g protein

✷ Ingredients

12 large square egg roll wrappers
2 cups shredded cabbage
1 cup chopped onions
½ cup shredded carrots
½ cup chopped bean sprouts
½ cup chopped celery
½ cup canned pineapple in juice, chopped
½ cup canned sliced water chestnuts, chopped
¼ cup light or low-sodium soy sauce
2 tablespoons minced garlic
Salt and black pepper, to taste

✷ Directions

Preheat oven to 350 degrees.

Place cabbage in a microwave-safe dish with 2 tablespoons of water and microwave for 3 minutes. Drain water and transfer cabbage to a large bowl.

Add all other ingredients to the bowl, except for the wrappers, and mix well. Season to taste with salt and black pepper. Set aside.

Place two egg roll wrappers on a clean, dry surface. Evenly place 2 heaping spoonfuls of the veggie mixture (1/12th of the total mixture) onto each wrapper, in rows a little below the center of each square. Moisten all four edges of each wrapper with water by dabbing your fingers in water and going over the edges smoothly.

Fold the sides of each wrapper about three-quarters of an inch toward the middle to keep the mixture from falling out of the sides. Then roll the bottom of each wrapper up around the mixture and continue rolling until you reach the top. Seal the outside edge once more with a dab of water.

Repeat process with all other wrappers, making sure you have a clean, dry surface each time. Place all of the egg rolls onto a large baking pan sprayed with nonstick spray.

Lightly spray the tops of the egg rolls with nonstick spray. Bake in the oven for about 25 minutes, until golden brown. Allow to cool slightly and then cut each egg roll in half.

MAKES 12 SERVINGS

For Weight Watchers **POINTS**®
values and photos of all the
recipes in this book, check out
hungry-girl.com/book.

chapter eight

chocolate 911

all things chocolate
kick your chocolate cravings to the curb.

Did you know that 50 percent of all food cravings are for chocolate? That's astounding, yet not at all surprising. This chapter is jam-packed with recipes that will help fulfill all of your chocolate dreams and satisfy any chocolate craving you might have—whether it's for cake, fudge, brownies . . . *whatever!* One word of advice: Do *not* eat all of these recipes, and go things at one time. That, of course, would be a terrible idea. But *do* have fun with these chocolate crazy!

chilly chocolate cheesecake nuggets

PER SERVING (2 nuggets): 42 calories, <0.5g fat, 130mg sodium, 7g carbs, 0g fiber, 2g sugars, 3g protein

✶ Ingredients

¾ cup Cool Whip Free
¼ cup plus 1 tablespoon fat-free cream cheese, softened
One 25-calorie packet diet hot cocoa mix
1 tablespoon sugar-free chocolate syrup
1 tablespoon Splenda No Calorie Sweetener (granulated)

✶ Directions

Using a fork or an electric mixer, vigorously mix Cool Whip, cream cheese, cocoa mix, syrup, and Splenda until smooth and well blended.

Evenly distribute mixture into 10 sections of an ice cube tray. Place tray in the freezer until nuggets are solid (at least 2 hours).

Once frozen, nuggets should pop out easily. (If not, run the bottom of the tray under the faucet for a few seconds to loosen them.)

MAKES 5 SERVINGS

HG SHOCKER!
Romano's Macaroni Grill serves up New York Cheesecake with Caramel Fudge sauce. It clocks in with an alarming 1,610 calories and 96 grams of fat—and that's just for *one slice*, not the entire cake!

dreamy chocolate peanut butter fudge

✳✳ *It may seem weird to use brownie mix to make faux fudge, but trust me—this recipe totally ROCKS!!!* ✳✳

✴ Ingredients

One 18.3-ounce box Betty Crocker Fudge Brownies Traditional Chewy Brownie Mix
2 cups canned pure pumpkin
2 tablespoons reduced-fat peanut butter, at room temperature

✴ Directions

Preheat oven to 350 degrees.

Combine pumpkin with the brownie mix in a large bowl and stir until smooth (batter will be very thick, but don't add anything else!).

Spray a square baking pan (9" x 9" works best) with nonstick spray and pour in the mixture. Spoon peanut butter on top and use a knife to swirl it around the top of the batter. Bake in the oven for 35 minutes. (The batter will remain very thick and fudgy, and it should look undercooked.) Allow to cool.

Cover pan with foil and place pan in the fridge for at least 2 hours. Cut into 36 squares.

MAKES 36 SERVINGS

Heads Up! *The Betty Crocker brownie mix used in this recipe is the best, since it's super-low in fat and contains fiber. Feel free to swap the stuff for your fave brownie mix, but nutritional information may vary.*

 For a pic of this recipe, see the photo insert. Yay!

chocolate-coated mousse-cream cones

PER SERVING (1 cone): 84 calories, 1g fat, 134mg sodium, 20g carbs, 0.5g fiber, 2g sugars, 1g protein

✳ Ingredients

2 cake/flat-bottom ice cream cones
1 Jell-O Sugar Free Pudding Snack (any flavor)
2 tablespoons sugar-free chocolate syrup,
    at fridge temperature
½ cup Cool Whip Free
Optional topping: additional sugar-free
    chocolate syrup

✳ Directions

Pour 1 tablespoon of chocolate syrup into each cone. Swirl around until the inside of each cone is evenly coated and then place cones in the freezer.

Place Cool Whip and pudding in a small dish and stir until blended. Chill dish in the freezer for 45 minutes to 1 hour, until mousse is ice cold and set but not fully frozen.

Remove cones and mousse mixture. Spoon mousse evenly into and on top of

cones. If desired, top each cone with a drizzle of chocolate syrup!

MAKES 2 SERVINGS

Heads Up! *After trying these, you may not crave ice cream ever again.*

CHEW ON THIS:

Chocolate syrup was used to represent blood in the famous 45-second shower scene in Alfred Hitchcock's movie *Psycho*.

HG Dilemma!

Are those candy bars worth the calories?

VICE: At the office, you grab one of those fun-sized candy bars from the bowl at the receptionist's desk—all 5 times you pass by it. (500 calories!)

PRICE: Like to tidy up? You'd have to organize your desk, straighten papers, and file documents for an additional 4 hours to get rid of those 500 calories!

Nutritional information based on averages.

pb 'n chocolate
bread pudding bonanza

✶✶ *Warning: This stuff's so good, it may make your head explode!* ✶✶

✶ Ingredients

3 slices light bread (40 to 45 calories each with about 2g fiber per slice), lightly toasted and cut into ½-inch cubes

1 cup light vanilla soymilk

⅓ cup fat-free liquid egg substitute

2 tablespoons reduced-fat peanut butter

2 tablespoons semi-sweet mini chocolate chips

2 tablespoons brown sugar (not packed)

Optional: fat-free whipped topping

✶ Directions

Preheat oven to 350 degrees.

Place toasted bread cubes into a 1-quart baking dish sprayed with nonstick spray and sprinkle chocolate chips evenly on top.

In a blender, combine soymilk, egg substitute, peanut butter, and brown sugar. Process at medium speed until smooth. Pour mixture over bread cubes, making sure all the bread cubes are covered. Let stand for 5 minutes.

Place dish in the oven and bake for 45 to 50 minutes, until pudding is firm.

This is best when served warm. If you like, add some whipped topping before serving.

MAKES 4 SERVINGS

 For a pic of this recipe, see the photo insert. Yay!

- -

CHEW ON THIS:

Chocolate contains the chemicals theobromine, methylxanthine, and phenylethylamine. These chemicals are known for their ability to produce a sense of happiness and well-being.

chilly chocolate mousse crepes

PER SERVING (1 crepe): 52 calories, 1g fat, 87mg sodium, 10g carbs, 0g fiber, 2g sugars, 2g protein

✳✳ *These don't always make it to the pan. They're pretty awesome straight from the freezer!* ✳✳

✳ Ingredients

2 ready-to-use dessert crepes (30 to 50 calories each)
1 Jell-O Chocolate Vanilla Swirl Sugar Free Pudding Snack
½ cup Cool Whip Free

✳ Directions

Place Cool Whip and pudding in a bowl and stir until blended.

Gently tear or cut each crepe in half. Into the center of each crepe half, spoon one-quarter of the pudding mixture. Fold crepes envelope style (sides in first), ensuring that there is nowhere for the mixture to seep out. Place crepes in the freezer for at least 1 hour.

Spray a pan with nonstick spray and heat over a medium-low flame. Beginning with the seam-sides facing up, heat crepes for 1 minute. Carefully turn crepes over and heat for an additional minute.

Crepes will be slightly browned 'n toasty on the outside, but cool 'n creamy on the inside!

MAKES 4 SERVINGS

HG Tip: Find ready-to-use dessert crepes in the produce section of the supermarket.

ooey gooey
chocolate cherry muffins

PER SERVING (1 muffin): 131 calories, <0.5g fat, 121mg sodium, 35g carbs, 3.5g fiber, 24g sugars, 3g protein

✸✸ *A box of No Pudge! Fat Free Fudge Brownie Mix is the perfect amount for this recipe. But feel free to use 12 servings (about 2⅔ cups) of another fat-free brownie mix.* ✸✸

✳ Ingredients

1 box No Pudge! Original Fat Free Fudge Brownie Mix
1 cup Fiber One bran cereal (original), crushed
⅔ cup light cherry pie filling
¼ cup light vanilla soymilk

✳ Directions

Preheat oven to 400 degrees.

In a bowl, mix all of the ingredients together. Place batter evenly into a 12-cup muffin pan sprayed with nonstick spray or lined with baking cups. Bake in the oven for 20 minutes.

MAKES 12 SERVINGS

For Weight Watchers *POINTS*® values and photos of all the recipes in this book, check out hungry-girl.com/book.

freakishly good frozen hot chocolate

PER SERVING (entire recipe): 58 calories, 0.5g fat, 184mg sodium, 10g carbs, 1g fiber, 5g sugars, 3g protein

✶ ✶ *This recipe was inspired by the world-famous (and insanely delicious) frozen hot chocolate served at NYC's Serendipity3.* ✶ ✶

✶ Ingredients

One 25-calorie packet diet hot cocoa mix
¼ cup light vanilla soymilk
½ ounce sugar-free calorie-free syrup (white chocolate or vanilla)
1 teaspoon sugar-free chocolate syrup
2 no-calorie sweetener packets
2 tablespoons Fat Free Reddi-wip
5 to 8 ice cubes *or* 1 cup crushed ice

✶ Directions

Place hot cocoa mix, chocolate syrup, and sweetener in a glass, and stir in 3 ounces of hot water. Next, add soymilk and sugar-free syrup and stir again. Place mix in the fridge or freezer for a few minutes or until cool.

Pour mix into a blender and add ice. Blend on the highest speed for about 45 seconds or until well blended. Pour into a tall mug. Finish off with whipped topping.

MAKES 1 SERVING

TOP ATE Health Benefits of Chocolate

"Ate" great reasons to indulge . . .

1. Dark chocolate is full of antioxidants, which can help lower blood pressure.

2. Heart-healthy flavonols promote blood flow.

3. Cocoa contains the same type of healthy monounsaturated fat found in olive oil (but tastes much better!).

4. Chocolate releases endorphins in the brain, which act as pain-relievers and stress-reducers.

5. Consuming chocolate releases serotonin in your body, which can boost your mood.

6. All those antioxidants help rid the body of free radicals, a fundamental cause of diseases like cancer and heart disease.

7. Studies show chocolate raises levels of the good cholesterol while reducing levels of the bad kind.

8. Essential oils found in cocoa can delay signs of aging—they strengthen your bones, hair, nails, and skin.

yum yum brownie muffins

✷✷ *It may seem odd to use nothing but pumpkin and cake mix for this recipe, but it works perfectly well. Hope you love it!* ✷✷

✶ Ingredients

1 box devil's food cake mix (about 18 ounces)
One 15-ounce can pure pumpkin

✶ Directions

Preheat oven to 400 degrees.

Mix the two ingredients together. Don't add anything else that may be mentioned on the box, like eggs, oil, or water. The mixture will be very thick, so you might be tempted to add in other things to make the batter smoother. Do *not* do this!

Place batter into a 12-cup muffin pan lined with baking cups or sprayed with nonstick spray. Place pan in the oven and bake for 20 minutes.

MAKES 12 SERVINGS

hot 'n nutty liquid brownie

✳ Ingredients

One 25-calorie packet diet hot cocoa mix
½ ounce sugar-free calorie-free hazelnut syrup
1 teaspoon semi-sweet mini chocolate chips
Optional: Fat Free Reddi-wip

✳ Directions

Bring 6 ounces of water to a near boil, either
on the stove or in the microwave. Set aside.

Place chocolate chips in a microwave-safe
mug, and microwave for 30 seconds or until
melted. Immediately add cocoa mix and hot
water and stir.

Next, pour in the hazelnut syrup and stir. If desired, top with
some whipped topping.

MAKES 1 SERVING

For Weight Watchers *POINTS*®
values and photos of all the
recipes in this book, check out
hungry-girl.com/book.

chocolate pudding crunch explosion

PER SERVING (entire recipe): 139 calories, 2.5g fat, 288mg sodium, 30g carbs, 1.5g fiber, 4g sugars, 4g protein

✳ Ingredients

1 Jell-O Sugar Free Chocolate Pudding Snack
3 caramel mini rice cakes or soy crisps, crushed
1 regular thin pretzel twist (or 4 minis), crushed
½ sheet (2 crackers) low-fat honey graham crackers, crushed
2 tablespoons Fat Free Reddi-wip

✳ Directions

Spoon pudding into a dish. Top with all of your crushed snacks. Add Reddi-wip and enjoy!

MAKES 1 SERVING

For a pic of this recipe, see the photo insert. Yay!

upside-down chocolate cream pie

PER SERVING (entire recipe): 135 calories, 2.5g fat, 280mg sodium, 30g carbs, 1.5g fiber, 5g sugars, 3g protein

✴ Ingredients

1 Jell-O Sugar Free Chocolate Pudding Snack
1 sheet (4 crackers) low-fat honey graham crackers, crushed
2 tablespoons Cool Whip Free

✴ Directions

Line the bottom of a small dish with whipped topping. Evenly spoon pudding on top. Cover with crushed graham cracker crumbs. Voilà!

MAKES 1 SERVING

CHEW ON THIS:

The average American consumes about 11.7 pounds of chocolate each year. That breaks down to about half an ounce a day (not too bad!).

death by chocolate cupcakes

✳ Ingredients

2 cups moist-style chocolate cake mix (½ of an 18.25-ounce box)
Two 25-calorie packets diet hot cocoa mix
½ cup fat-free liquid egg substitute
2 tablespoons semi-sweet mini chocolate chips
1 teaspoon Splenda No Calorie Sweetener (granulated)
⅛ teaspoon salt

✳ Directions

Place chocolate chips and the contents of both cocoa packets in a tall glass. Add 12 ounces of boiling water and stir until chips and cocoa mix have dissolved. Place glass in the freezer to chill for 25 minutes.

Preheat oven to 350 degrees.

Once cocoa has chilled, give it a stir and mix with all other ingredients in a mixing bowl. Whip batter with a whisk or fork for 2 minutes.

Spray a 12-cup muffin pan with nonstick spray or line it with baking cups. Evenly spoon batter (which will be thin, but don't worry—your cupcakes will puff up!) into the pan. Place pan in the oven and

HG SHOCKER!
If you find yourself craving chocolate while shopping at Costco, don't break down and devour their Kirkland Chocolate Muffin. That hunk of cocoa-y fat 'n flour will set you back 690 calories and 38 grams of fat.

bake for 15 minutes. Cupcakes will look shiny when done.

MAKES 12 SERVINGS

. . . .

Would You Rather . . .

An average fudge nut brownie dessert has 650 calories. To burn all those calories, you'd have to:

* ✳ Jump rope furiously for an hour nonstop *or*
* ✳ Do 2 hours of heavy gardening (hedge trimming included) *or*
* ✳ Spend 4 hours ironing extra-wrinkly button-downs!

Times based on estimates for a 150-pound woman.

chapter
nine

fruity call

food with fruit
all fruit, all the time.

Fruit is totally natural, packed with fiber, inexpensive, and 100 percent bad-cholesterol-free. It helps stimulate memory, has healing effects, and tastes *great*. Could you possibly need more reasons than that to eat it? How about a bunch of awesome HG creations like fruit slaw, fruit salsa, and indulgent and creamy, fruity desserts? These recipes will rock your fruit-loving face off!

topless triple berry pie

✳ Ingredients

1½ cups frozen strawberries
¾ cup frozen blueberries
¼ cup frozen raspberries
2 cups Fiber One bran cereal (original)
¼ cup light whipped butter or light buttery spread, melted and mixed with
    1 ounce water
4 no-calorie sweetener packets
1 tablespoon cornstarch
1 tablespoon Splenda No Calorie Sweetener (granulated)
1 teaspoon cinnamon
¼ teaspoon vanilla extract
Optional: fat-free whipped topping

✳ Directions

Preheat oven to 350 degrees.

In a blender or food processor, grind Fiber One to a breadcrumb-like consistency. Combine crumbs with butter mixture, cinnamon, and the contents of the sweetener packets. Stir until well mixed.

In an oven-safe 9-inch pie dish sprayed lightly with nonstick spray, evenly distribute mixture, using your hands or a flat utensil to firmly press and form the crust. Press it into the edges and up along the sides of the dish.

Bake crust in the oven for 10 minutes and then remove it and allow to cool.

In a medium pot, heat berries over a medium flame until they are mostly thawed. Add Splenda, cornstarch, and vanilla extract. Mix well.

Once mixture is thoroughly heated and begins to bubble, reduce heat to low and continue to cook, stirring occasionally, for 5 minutes or until mixture has thickened. Then remove pot from heat and allow it to cool for several minutes.

Once berry mix has cooled, evenly spoon it into the pie crust. Allow pie to cool and set in the fridge for several hours before cutting.

Cut pie into 8 slices. If desired, top each slice with fat-free whipped topping before serving.

MAKES 8 SERVINGS

HG Tip: Pick up one of those frozen bags of mixed berries and your pie will practically make itself!

CHEW ON THIS:

Blueberries contain more antioxidants than most other fruits. And they won't ripen once they're picked!

bananarama wafer puddin'

PER SERVING (½ cup): 137 calories, 1.5g fat, 299mg sodium, 29g carbs, 1g fiber, 15g sugars, 4g protein

✳ Ingredients

2 cups fat-free milk, at fridge temperature
2 medium bananas, sliced
24 Reduced Fat Nilla Wafers
1 small (4 serving) package sugar-free fat-free instant vanilla pudding mix
Optional: fat-free whipped topping

✳ Directions

Combine pudding mix and milk in a bowl. Beat with a whisk for 2 minutes or until thoroughly blended. Set aside.

In a medium bowl or casserole dish, arrange a layer of wafers and then top with a layer of banana slices. Continue alternating layers until all wafers and banana slices are in the dish.

Top dish with the pudding and let it seep down in between the wafer and banana layers. Refrigerate for 2 to 3 hours. If desired, add whipped topping before serving.

MAKES 6 SERVINGS

apple cinnamon crunch parfaits

PER SERVING (1 parfait): 135 calories, 0.5g fat, 101mg sodium, 30g carbs, 1.5g fiber, 20g sugars, 5g protein

✳ Ingredients

6 ounces fat-free vanilla yogurt

1½ cups peeled and chopped apples

7 caramel mini rice cakes or soy crisps, crushed

1 tablespoon Splenda No Calorie Sweetener (granulated)

2 teaspoons cornstarch

½ teaspoon cinnamon

¼ teaspoon vanilla extract

Optional: fat-free whipped topping

✳ Directions

Place apple chunks in a microwave-safe dish with ¼ cup of water and cover. Microwave for 2½ minutes. Drain water and set aside.

Mix Splenda, cornstarch, cinnamon, and vanilla extract into ½ cup of cold water. In a saucepan over medium-low heat, cook and stir liquid mixture until thickened to a caramel-sauce-like consistency (add a few drops more water if sauce becomes too thick). Remove from heat and stir apples into the mixture. Allow to cool and set for several minutes (for a warm parfait) or refrigerate until cold.

Once ready to serve, layer apple mixture, yogurt, and crushed rice cakes (or soy crisps) evenly into 2 cups. Add a little whipped topping, if you like.

MAKES 2 SERVINGS

fruity super-slaw

This recipe was co-developed with Weight Watchers®.

✳ Ingredients

4 cups shredded green cabbage
3½ cups shredded purple cabbage
1 cup thinly sliced 1-inch jicama strips
1 medium Granny Smith apple
1 cup red grapes
½ cup white wine vinegar
½ cup grape juice concentrate
2½ ounces fat-free raspberry yogurt
2 tablespoons fat-free mayonnaise
2 tablespoons sugar
½ teaspoon lime juice
½ teaspoon salt
⅛ teaspoon pepper

✳ Directions

Stir to combine vinegar, grape juice concentrate, and sugar with 3 cups of water.

Place shredded cabbage and jicama in a bowl, and cover with vinegar mixture. Stir thoroughly, cover, and then allow to marinate in the fridge for 1 hour. After 1 hour, stir mixture and return to the fridge for 10 to 15 minutes.

Meanwhile, thinly slice apple into 1-inch strips and cut grapes in half. In a small dish, combine yogurt, mayo, lime juice, salt, and pepper. Mix well.

Remove slaw from fridge and add one tablespoon of its marinade to the yogurt mixture, stir until blended.

Next, strain slaw thoroughly (draining *all* of the remaining marinade) and then return slaw to the bowl. Add fruit and yogurt dressing, and toss until completely mixed.

MAKES 8 SERVINGS

CHEW ON THIS:

Strawberries are the *only* fruit that have their seeds on the outside. Fancy!

groovy grilled fruit fondue

PER SERVING (¼th of recipe): 135 calories, 0.5g fat, 98mg sodium, 30g carbs, 3g fiber, 22g sugars, 6g protein

✳ ✳ *This fruit fondue is a really fun addition to any dinner party. Just wanted to put that out there . . .* ✳ ✳

✳ Ingredients

1 medium Granny Smith apple

1 large firm nectarine

1 small slightly under-ripe banana

1 cup fresh pineapple chunks

12 ounces fat-free vanilla yogurt

2 tablespoons fat-free cream cheese, softened

2 teaspoons Splenda No Calorie Sweetener (granulated)

1 teaspoon cinnamon

✳ Directions

Cut all fruit into large, bite-sized chunks. In a pan sprayed with nonstick spray (or on the grill if you have one), grill fruit over medium-high heat for about 4 minutes, flipping fruit halfway through. Fruit should be slightly browned on the outside, but still firm inside.

In a microwave-safe bowl, combine yogurt, cream cheese, Splenda, and cinnamon. Heat for 45 seconds in the microwave. Stir and then microwave for an additional 40 seconds. Serve fruit and cheese sauce with skewers or fondue sticks for easy dipping!

MAKES 4 SERVINGS

apple pie pockets

PER SERVING (1 pocket): 137 calories, 0.5g fat, 146mg sodium, 33g carbs, 4.5g fiber, 16g sugars, 3g protein

✶ Ingredients

4 medium apples, peeled and sliced

2 whole wheat (or high-fiber) pitas, halved and heated

1 tablespoon brown sugar (not packed)

2 teaspoons cornstarch

½ teaspoon cinnamon

¼ teaspoon vanilla extract

✶ Directions

In a small covered saucepan, cook apples over medium heat in ¼ cup of water until tender (2 to 3 minutes). Remove from heat and drain water. Remove apples from the pan and set them aside.

Mix brown sugar, cornstarch, cinnamon, and vanilla extract with ¼ cup of cold water. Cook and stir mixture in saucepan over medium-low heat, until thickened to a caramel-sauce-like consistency, adding a few drops more water if it gets too thick.

Remove from heat and stir apples into the mixture. Stuff each pita half with one-quarter of the mixture.

MAKES 4 SERVINGS

layered berry custard crostata

PER SERVING (½ of crostata): 124 calories, 1.5g fat, 170mg sodium, 26g carbs, 3.5g fiber, 4g sugars, 2g protein

✴✴ *This layered berry custard treat is so good, we were laughing uncontrollably the first time we ate it at the HG HQ. There is absolutely no way anyone would ever know or believe how low in calories and fat it is!* ✴✴

✴ Ingredients

Two 9" x 14" sheets phyllo dough, thawed according to package directions
1 Jell-O Sugar Free Vanilla Pudding Snack
¾ cup blackberries and raspberries
½ cup Cool Whip Free

✴ Directions

Preheat oven to 350 degrees.

Spray each sheet of phyllo dough with nonstick spray and place on top of one another on a clean, dry cutting board. Slice sheets into three long pieces and stack them on top of one another. Cut sheets once more into two rectangular stacks. Gently place them next to one another on a baking pan sprayed with nonstick spray.

Place pan in the oven and cook for 5 minutes. Meanwhile, mix together pudding and Cool Whip. Remove phyllo dough from the oven and let it cool for a few minutes.

Spread half of pudding mixture over one stack of dough and place half of the berries on top. Place second phyllo stack carefully on top of the berry layer and spread on the rest of the pudding mix. Top with remaining berries.

MAKES 2 SERVINGS

Share this ginormous dessert with a friend, family member, or dog you like a lot.

Heads Up! The phyllo dough is a bit tricky to work with, but this recipe ROCKS, so it's worth the trouble.

For a pic of this recipe, see the photo insert. Yay!

Fruity 411 . . .

* Cherries may help you sleep better! They're rich in melatonin, a powerful antioxidant known for regulating the body's natural sleep cycle.

* Apples are packed with two types of fiber, and when these insoluble and soluble fibers join forces they can actually lower your cholesterol.

* Cranberries have been long known to provide protection against urinary tract and kidney infections.

* Grapes have been found to combat heart problems and can actually strengthen muscles in the heart.

sweetie-fry bananas
with cream cheese frosting

✴✴ *Fried bananas with sweet cream cheese frosting for only about 200 calories and 1 gram of fat?! That is complete insanity. BTW, this dessert also packs in a whopping 10.5 grams of fiber!!!* ✴✴

✴ Ingredients

1 large banana
¼ cup Fiber One bran cereal (original)
3 tablespoons Cool Whip Free
2 tablespoons Splenda No Calorie Sweetener (granulated), divided
1 tablespoon fat-free cream cheese, softened
⅛ teaspoon cinnamon
Dash of salt

✴ Directions

To create the cream cheese frosting, combine cream cheese, Cool Whip, and half of the Splenda. Stir until smooth. Place mix in the fridge to chill.

In a food processor or blender, combine Fiber One, cinnamon, salt, and the remaining tablespoon of Splenda, and blend until a breadcrumb-like consistency is achieved.

Cut banana in half widthwise and then lengthwise, so you have 4 pieces. Spray banana pieces (both sides) with nonstick spray. Roll banana pieces in the "breadcrumb" mixture, making sure to cover them entirely.

Cook banana slices in a pan sprayed with nonstick spray, over medium heat, for 3 to 4 minutes per side, until crispy. Serve with chilled cream cheese frosting.

MAKES 1 SERVING

CHEW ON THIS:

Bananas are the most popular fruit in America. Americans eat 33 pounds of bananas per person per year . . . Yowsa!

cheery cherry cobbler

PER SERVING (¼th of cobbler): 156 calories, 1g fat, 150mg sodium, 36g carbs, 3g fiber, 21g sugars, 3g protein

✳ Ingredients

3 cups halved and pitted sweet cherries, fresh or thawed if frozen
4 sheets (16 crackers) low-fat honey graham crackers
2 tablespoons fat-free liquid egg substitute
2 tablespoons no-sugar-added applesauce
2 tablespoons Splenda No Calorie Sweetener (granulated), divided
1 tablespoon brown sugar (not packed)
1 tablespoon cornstarch
1 teaspoon cinnamon
Dash of salt

✳ Directions

Preheat oven to 400 degrees.

Combine ⅔ cup of cold water with brown sugar, cornstarch, salt, and half of the Splenda, stir well. In a medium pot, combine cherries with this mixture.

Heat cherry mixture over medium heat, stirring often. Once liquid thickens to a syrupy consistency and begins to bubble, reduce heat to low and cover. Allow to simmer for 5 minutes and then transfer cherry mixture to a medium round baking dish. Set aside.

Next, break graham crackers into pieces and crush them (either in a food processor or blender, or by placing cracker pieces in a sealable plastic bag and crushing them with a rolling pin on the bag). Transfer crumbs to a microwave-safe dish and add egg substitute, applesauce, cinnamon, and remaining tablespoon of Splenda. Stir well.

Microwave cracker mixture for 1 minute. Use a fork to break up the toughened mixture as much as possible and then allow to cool for a few minutes.

Transfer cracker mixture to a food processor or blender and pulse until crumbly and uniform. Evenly distribute graham cracker topping over cherries.

Place the dish in the oven and bake for 10 minutes. Allow to cool slightly before serving.

MAKES 4 SERVINGS

bestest baked apples

PER SERVING (1 apple): 72 calories, <0.5g fat, 10mg sodium, 19g carbs, 3g fiber, 14g sugars, 0g protein

✶ ✶ *These baked apples are CLASSIC! And they're great alone or with low-fat cottage cheese, low-fat ice cream, frozen yogurt, or regular yogurt. Yum!* ✶ ✶

✶ Ingredients

4 medium Rome apples
1 can diet black cherry soda
½ no-calorie sweetener packet
Dash of cinnamon

✶ Directions

Preheat oven to 375 degrees.

Core apples. Place in a casserole dish. Pour the entire can of soda over apples. Sprinkle cinnamon and sweetener over apples.

Place dish in the oven and bake for 45 minutes or until apples are tender. Serve warm, hot, or cold.

MAKES 4 SERVINGS

For Weight Watchers *POINTS*® values and photos of all the recipes in this book, check out hungry-girl.com/book.

TOP ATE Fiber-Packed Fruits!
The most fiber-happy fruits in the world . . .

1. Dates—A cup of pitted dates contains 14 grams of fiber!

2. Avocado—Sliced avocado has a whopping 10 grams of fiber per cup.

3. Guava—9 grams of fiber in each cup of groovy guava.

4. Raspberries—A cup of raspberries serves up 8 grams of fiber.

5. Blackberries—A cup of blackberries follows with 7.5 grams of fiber.

6. Kiwi—Kiwi slices contain more than 5 grams of fiber per cup.

7. Cranberries/Pears—We know this is a Top "Ate," but both whole cranberries and sliced pears contain 4 to 5 grams of fiber per cup!

8. Blueberries—You'll take in 3.5 grams of fiber from each cup of blueberries you chew.

CHEW ON THIS:

If you want your fruit to ripen quicker, place it in a paper bag and let it sit out at room temperature. Remember to check it often!

super-simple tropical sorbet

PER SERVING (entire recipe): 76 calories, <0.5g fat, 0mg sodium, 16g carbs, 2.5g fiber, 14g sugars, 2g protein

✳✳ *Try experimenting with lots of fruits and drink mix flavors for endless sorbet options!* ✳✳

✳ Ingredients

1 packet (two 5-calorie servings) sugar-free powdered orange drink mix
1 cup sliced peaches, fresh, thawed if frozen, or drained and rinsed if canned

✳ Directions

Dissolve drink mix into 4 ounces of cold water, stir well. In a blender, puree peaches and drink mixture until just blended.

Pour mixture into a dish, cover, and place in freezer until nearly solid (several hours). If freezing overnight, thaw sorbet slightly by microwaving for 30 to 40 seconds or allowing to sit out for about 10 minutes before serving.

MAKES 1 SERVING

ice creamless banana split

PER SERVING (entire recipe): 157 calories, 2g fat, 10mg sodium, 41g carbs, 2.5g fiber, 17g sugars, 1g protein

✷✷ *Yeah, it's unconventional (and maybe even a bit nervy) to put a banana split recipe in here that doesn't call for ice cream. But it's REALLY good. And fun!!!* ✷✷

✷ Ingredients

1 small banana
3 tablespoons Cool Whip Free, frozen
2 tablespoons sugar-free strawberry preserves
1 teaspoon semi-sweet mini chocolate chips

✷ Directions

Slice banana in half, first lengthwise and then widthwise. Place banana pieces in a bowl.

In a separate dish, mix strawberry preserves with 1 tablespoon of hot water to create a strawberry syrup. Pour strawberry syrup over bananas.

Top with Cool Whip Free and then sprinkle chocolate chips on top. Enjoy!

MAKES 1 SERVING

fiesta tropical fruit salsa

PER SERVING (½ cup): 46 calories, <0.5g fat, 29mg sodium, 12g carbs, 1.5g fiber, 9g sugars, 1g protein

✳ Ingredients

1¼ cups diced mango
1¼ cups diced pineapple
⅓ cup diced red onions
⅓ cup diced red bell peppers
3 tablespoons sliced scallions
3 tablespoons chopped fresh cilantro
3 tablespoons lime juice
Dash of salt

✳ Directions

In a medium bowl, stir together all of the ingredients. Cover and refrigerate for at least 1 hour.

MAKES 6 SERVINGS

HG Tip: *The great thing about this recipe is that it is easy to tweak it to suit your taste buds! Like tomato-based salsa? Add a cup of tomatoes! Like an even fruitier topping for your chicken or fish? Try adding kiwi or honeydew melon!*

Pick Me! Pick Me!

How to pick the *best* fruit . . .

Pineapple–Pineapples should be brightly colored with fresh-looking, deep green leaves, and should be free of bruises and moldy spots (ew!). They should also have a sweet smell at the stem. FYI, a ripe, uncut pineapple will last for about 4 days at room temperature or in the fridge.

Apples–Color has nothing to do with how ripe or unripe an apple is. Bruise-free apples are best. Also, don't wash apples until you're about to eat them. Believe it or not, washing apples makes them spoil faster.

Peaches–Choose a peach with an orangy-red color, as opposed to one with a yellowish hue. If you can gently squeeze the peach without breaking the skin, it is ripe and ready to eat. If you choose a hard peach, it will ripen in a few days. And remember, peaches bruise super-easily, so take special care when handling them.

Avocado–Yep, avocado is a fruit. When looking to choose a ripe avocado, gently squeeze it. There should be a little bit of give. If you squeeze it and end up with a handful of guacamole, your bumpy friend is over-ripe!

chapter
ter

oven lovin'

baked goods and other treats
no-guilt desserts? sweet!

Just in case there weren't enough sweet treats for you in the chocolate and fruit chapters, here are tons of others. You'll find crazy-good breakfast breads, frozen treats, crunchy stuff, and more. And you'll be happy to know that not everything in this chapter requires you to use an oven. There are plenty of super-simple recipes that require no heating at all. Dig in and enjoy!!!

snazzy blueberry scones

PER SERVING (1 scone): 125 calories, 2.5g fat, 181mg sodium, 23g carbs, 2g fiber, 6g sugars, 4g protein

✷✷ *These scones are really fantastic and can be made in so many flavors. All you need to do is swap blueberries for some other fruit, like peaches or strawberries. Yum!* ✷✷

✶ Ingredients

⅔ cup regular oats (not instant)
⅓ cup Bisquick Heart Smart baking mix
¾ cup blueberries
⅓ cup light vanilla soymilk
1 tablespoon brown sugar (not packed)
2 teaspoons light whipped butter or light buttery spread, softened
½ teaspoon baking powder

✶ Directions

Preheat oven to 400 degrees.

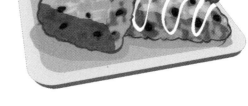

Combine dry ingredients with butter and mix well. Add milk and stir. Then fold berries into the batter.

On a baking pan sprayed with nonstick spray, divide batter into 4 mounds (leave room in between 'em—they expand!).

Bake for 10 minutes.

MAKES 4 SERVINGS

tremendous tiramisu

PER SERVING (entire recipe): 220 calories, 2.5g fat, 275mg sodium, 38g carbs, 2g fiber, 20g sugars, 11g protein

✳ Ingredients

6 soft ladyfingers

½ cup strong-brewed flavored coffee (or espresso), cooled and sweetened, to taste, with no-calorie sweetener

¼ cup fat-free ricotta cheese

2 tablespoons Cool Whip Free

1 tablespoon unsweetened cocoa powder, divided

1 teaspoon Splenda No Calorie Sweetener (granulated)

½ teaspoon vanilla extract

✳ Directions

Line up 3 of the ladyfingers next to each other on a serving dish. Drizzle as much as half of the cooled coffee over ladyfingers, until desired saturation is reached.

In a small bowl, combine ricotta cheese, Splenda, Cool Whip, and vanilla extract. Mix well. Spread half of the mixture on top of ladyfingers. Top with half of the cocoa.

Next, layer remaining ladyfingers on top. Again, saturate with coffee. Spread remaining cheese mixture on top.

Sprinkle the rest of the cocoa over the dish and serve immediately.

MAKES 1 SERVING

caramel pumpkin pudding cupcakes

PER SERVING (1 cupcake): 108 calories, 2g fat, 188mg sodium, 21g carbs, 0.5g fiber, 12g sugars, 2g protein

✷✷ *These cupcakes are insanely fantastic! Even if you aren't a huge fan of pumpkin, you'll FLIP over 'em! And if you ARE a pumpkin-lover, you MUST visit the pumpkin section in the "Fun With . . ." chapter on page 268!* ✷✷

✶ Ingredients

For Cupcakes
2 cups moist-style yellow cake mix (½ of an 18.25-ounce box)
1 cup canned pure pumpkin
⅓ cup fat-free liquid egg substitute
2 tablespoons sugar-free maple syrup
2 teaspoons cinnamon
2 teaspoons Splenda No Calorie Sweetener (granulated)
⅛ teaspoon salt

For Topping
3 cubes (about 1 ounce) chewy caramel
2 teaspoons light vanilla soymilk

✶ Directions

Preheat oven to 350 degrees.

Combine all cupcake ingredients in a mixing bowl with ⅓ cup of water. Whip with a whisk or fork for 2 minutes until well blended.

Spray a 12-cup muffin pan with nonstick spray or line with baking cups. Evenly spoon batter into muffin cups. Place pan in the oven and cook for about 12 minutes (until cupcakes have puffed up but still appear a little gooey on top).

Once cupcakes are cool enough to handle, arrange them closely on a plate so that the edges are touching.

Place caramel and soymilk in a tall microwave-safe glass or dish (mixture will bubble and rise when heated). Microwave at medium power for 1½ minutes. Stir mixture vigorously until smooth and thoroughly blended. (Return to microwave for 30 seconds at medium heat if caramel has not fully melted.) Immediately drizzle caramel sauce over cupcakes.

MAKES 12 SERVINGS

📷 For a pic of this recipe, see the photo insert. Yay!

CHEW ON THIS:

Pumpkins are 90 percent water. No wonder they're so low in calories!

peach-blueberry oatmeal muffinmania

✳ Ingredients

1½ cups regular oats (not instant)
½ cup flour (not packed)
2 Jell-O Sugar Free Vanilla Pudding Snacks
1 cup canned peaches in juice, drained and chopped
½ cup blueberries
½ cup fat-free liquid egg substitute
3 tablespoons light vanilla soymilk
2 tablespoons light whipped butter or light buttery spread
¼ cup plus 2 tablespoons dark brown sugar (not packed)
2 teaspoons baking powder
½ teaspoon cinnamon
¼ teaspoon salt

✳ Directions

Preheat oven to 375 degrees.

Combine oats, flour, sugar, baking powder, cinnamon, and salt in a large bowl and stir well.

In a separate bowl, combine pudding, butter, soymilk, and egg substitute. Blend well with a whisk.

Add pudding mixture to dry mixture, stirring until just blended. Slowly fold in peaches and blueberries.

Divide mixture evenly into a 12-cup muffin pan sprayed with nonstick spray or lined with baking cups. Bake for 18 minutes or until a toothpick inserted in the center comes out clean.

MAKES 12 SERVINGS

· ·

The 411 on Bread-y Breakfast Treats

Some of these stats may surprise you . . .

English Muffin—130 calories and 1g fat

Plain Bagel—290 calories and 2g fat

Donut—200 calories and 10g fat

Scone—400 calories and 16g fat

Muffin—450 calories and 15g fat

Nutritional information based on averages.

peaches 'n cream pie

PER SERVING (1 slice): 85 calories, 3g fat, 158mg sodium, 17g carbs, 7g fiber, 1.5g sugars, 2g protein

✴ Ingredients

2 cups Fiber One bran cereal (original)
¼ cup light whipped butter or light buttery spread, melted
1 large 8-serving box (or 2 small 4-serving boxes)
    Jell-O Sugar Free Peach Gelatin Dessert Mix
1½ cups Cool Whip Free
Optional: sliced peaches (for garnish)

✴ Directions

Preheat oven to 350 degrees.

In a large bowl, dissolve gelatin mix into 2 cups of boiling water. Stir for 2 minutes or until completely dissolved. Then stir in 1 cup of cold water and place in the fridge for about 1½ hours (but not longer than that—the mixture should be thickened but not gelled).

Meanwhile, in a blender or food processor, grind Fiber One to a breadcrumb-like consistency. Combine crumbs with melted butter and stir until well mixed.

In an oven-safe pie dish sprayed with nonstick spray, evenly distribute Fiber One mixture, using your hands or a flat utensil to press and form the crust. Use your fingers to press it into the edges and up along the sides of the dish. Bake pie crust in the oven for 10 minutes. Set aside.

Once Jell-O has thickened, use an electric mixer to blend in the Cool Whip. When mixture is uniform and smooth, pour it evenly into the pie crust. Use a flat utensil to smooth out the surface. Refrigerate for several hours until firm. If desired, garnish pie with peach slices. Cut into 8 slices.

MAKES 8 SERVINGS

. . . .

TOP ATE Toppings for Frozen Yogurt, Sorbet, and Light Ice Cream

In search of toppings? These ROCK!

1. Fat Free Reddi-wip (2 tablespoons = 5 calories, 0g fat)

2. Sprinkles/Jimmies (1 teaspoon = 20 calories, 1g fat)

3. Sliced Strawberries (5 medium berries = 20 calories, <0.5g fat)

4. Crushed Caramel-Flavored Soy Crisps or Mini Rice Cakes (4 crisps or mini cakes = 30 calories, <0.5g fat)

5. Sugar-Free Strawberry Preserves (2 tablespoons = 20 calories, 0g fat)

6. Crushed Cone Pieces (1 cake/flat-bottom cone = 20 calories, <0.5g fat)

7. Mini Marshmallows (10 marshmallows = 20 calories, 0g fat)

8. Hot Cinnamon & Splenda-Topped Apple Slices (½ cup = 35 calories, <0.5g fat)

coconut patty pudding

✳✳ *This pudding is great and can be made in a variety of delicious flavor combos. You can get really creative with light vanilla soymilk and fruity sugar-free syrups!* ✳✳

✳ Ingredients

1½ cups light chocolate soymilk
2 ounces sugar-free calorie-free coconut syrup
2 tablespoons cornstarch
1 teaspoon Splenda No Calorie Sweetener (granulated)
Optional: fat-free whipped topping

✳ Directions

Combine all ingredients in a medium saucepan. Stir well and then set stove to medium heat.

Stirring constantly, allow mixture to reach a boil (about 5 minutes). Once mixture has thickened and begun to boil, remove from heat.

Spoon mixture into three dishes. Place them in the fridge for several hours, until pudding has set.

If desired, top each dish with some whipped topping before serving.

MAKES 3 SERVINGS

krispymallow treats

PER SERVING (1 piece): 46 calories, 1g fat, 32mg sodium, 11g carbs, 2.5g fiber, 4g sugars, 1g protein

✳ ✳ *If you LOVE Rice Krispies Treats, you'll flip over this fiber-packed version!* ✳ ✳

✳ Ingredients

5 cups puffed wheat cereal
2 cups Fiber One bran cereal (original)
3 cups miniature marshmallows
3 tablespoons light whipped butter or light buttery spread

✳ Directions

Melt butter in a large saucepan over low heat. Add marshmallows and stir until completely melted. Remove from heat.

Add both cereals. Stir until thoroughly coated.

Using a spatula, press mixture evenly into a 9" x 13" baking pan sprayed with nonstick spray. Allow to cool. Cut into 25 squares.

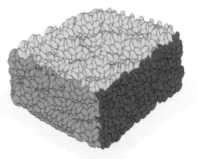

MAKES 25 SERVINGS

maris's big bowl o' blob orange 'n cream dessert

PER SERVING (¼th of bowl): 50 calories, 0.5g fat, 157mg sodium, 6g carbs, 0g fiber, 2g sugars, 2g protein

✷✷ *This crazy stuff was invented by our friend Maris (who is actually the mom of an HG staffer). It's a fizzy, creamy, wobbly dream dessert and can be used in parfaits, as pie filling, or eaten straight from the bowl! Feel free to experiment with a slew of SF Jell-O and diet soda flavors!* ✷✷

✷ Ingredients

1 cup Cool Whip Free
1 large 8-serving box (or 2 small 4-serving boxes) Jell-O Sugar Free Orange Gelatin Dessert Mix
1 can diet cream soda

✷ Directions

Dissolve gelatin mix into 2 cups of boiling water. Stir for 2 minutes or until completely dissolved. Then stir in soda.

Refrigerate for about 1½ hours (mixture should be thickened, but not gelled).

With an electric mixer, stir in Cool Whip until thoroughly blended. Return to fridge until very firm (overnight is best).

MAKES 4 SERVINGS

For Weight Watchers **POINTS**®
values and photos of all the
recipes in this book, check out
hungry-girl.com/book.

upside-down coconut-y cream pie

PER SERVING (entire recipe): 124 calories, 3.5g fat, 243mg sodium, 24g carbs, 1.5g fiber, 6g sugars, 3g protein

✴ Ingredients

1 Jell-O Sugar Free Vanilla Pudding Snack
½ sheet (2 crackers) low-fat honey graham crackers, crushed
¼ teaspoon coconut extract
1 tablespoon sweetened coconut flakes
2 tablespoons Fat Free Reddi-wip

✴ Directions

Spoon pudding into a small bowl. Mix in coconut extract.

Top pudding with crushed graham crackers and coconut flakes. Finish off this creamy coconut cloud with whipped topping. Mmmmm.

MAKES 1 SERVING

CHEW ON THIS:

Not only is coconut delicious, it's good for you, too. It's packing fiber, vitamins, and minerals. (Just don't overeat it—it's fairly high in calories!)

strawberry cheesecake minis

PER SERVING (1 cheesecake mini): 65 calories, 1g fat,
229mg sodium, 9g carbs, 0g fiber, 1g sugars, 7g protein

✳ ✳ *These mini cheesecakes taste best when eaten the day they're prepared!.* ✳ ✳

✳ Ingredients

For Cheesecakes
16 ounces fat-free cream cheese, softened
2 sheets (8 crackers) low-fat honey graham crackers
¼ cup fat-free egg substitute
¼ cup light vanilla soymilk
½ cup Splenda No Calorie Sweetener (granulated)
2 teaspoons Coffee-mate Fat Free French Vanilla powdered creamer,
    dissolved in 1 tablespoon warm water
1¾ teaspoons unflavored gelatin (most of a ¼-ounce envelope)
1½ teaspoons vanilla extract

For Topping
½ cup sugar-free strawberry preserves
¼ teaspoon unflavored gelatin (remaining contents of the ¼-ounce envelope)

✳ Directions

Preheat oven to 350 degrees.

Break graham crackers into small pieces and place in a sealable plastic bag.
Using a rolling pin (or any smooth cylindrical kitchen container), crush crackers
until reduced to crumbs. Line a 12-cup muffin pan with baking cups and evenly

distribute crumbs among them; shake pan so crumbs settle evenly along the bottom of each cup. Place pan in oven for 5 minutes and then remove.

Dissolve 1¾ teaspoons of the gelatin into ¼ cup of boiling water. Stir vigorously until the mixture is free of granules and lumps. Set aside.

Place cream cheese in a large mixing bowl. In a separate container, combine all other cheesecake ingredients, including gelatin mixture. Using an electric mixer on low speed, slowly blend liquid mixture into cream cheese. Raise mixer speed to medium-high and blend until mixture is uniform and free of lumps. Evenly spoon mixture into muffin pan and bake in the oven for about 15 minutes (until tops begin to crack).

Meanwhile, combine topping ingredients and stir well. Once cheesecakes are done cooking, remove pan from the oven. Evenly distribute topping among the centers of the tops of the cheesecakes, avoiding the edges. Return pan to the oven for 5 minutes.

Allow pan to cool for 20 minutes, then refrigerate until chilled (at least 3 hours). For best results, keep refrigerated until ready to serve.

MAKES 12 SERVINGS

upside-down
bananaberry crumble

PER SERVING (½ of recipe): 140 calories, 1.5g fat, 174mg sodium, 32g carbs, 3g fiber, 14g sugars, 2g protein

✳ Ingredients

1 medium banana, sliced

¾ cup chopped strawberries

2 sheets (8 crackers) low-fat honey graham crackers, crushed

1 tablespoon Splenda No Calorie Sweetener (granulated)

½ teaspoon imitation rum extract

¼ teaspoon cornstarch

Dash of salt

Optional: fat-free whipped topping

✳ Directions

Preheat oven to 450 degrees.

In a small dish, combine Splenda, rum extract, cornstarch, and salt with 1 tablespoon of water. Stir well.

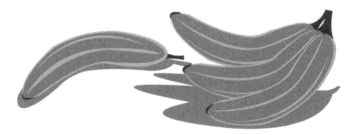

Place banana slices and strawberries in a separate dish. Cover with liquid mixture and stir.

Pour fruit mixture into a mini loaf pan (about 6" x 3") sprayed with nonstick spray. Evenly top with the crushed graham crackers.

Place pan in the oven and bake for about 12 minutes or until cracker topping begins to brown.

To serve, place a plate over the loaf pan and then swiftly flip upside down. Wiggle the dessert out of the dish and enjoy! If desired, top with whipped topping.

MAKES 2 SERVINGS

. . . .

Just Desserts!

Need something sweet while eating out? Making smart choices can help you save BIG. Here's proof . . .

Strawberry Shortcake vs. Berries and Cream

FIGHT IT! Strawberry Shortcake can easily contain 600+ calories and 25+ grams of fat.

BITE IT! Opt for a bowl of berries and a little whipped cream, and you'll typically take in under 120 calories and WAY less fat. This simple switch saves you about 500 calories!

Ice Cream Sundae vs. Fruit Sorbet

FIGHT IT! Need something sweet and chilly? Polish off an ice cream sundae and you'll have swallowed 550 calories and 25 grams of fat.

BITE IT! Get your hands on some fruit sorbet instead. If you eat a cup of sorbet, it will likely contain only about 250 calories and no fat.

Chocolate Cream Pie vs. Hot Cocoa

FIGHT IT! That slice of chocolate cream pie looks delicious, but is it worth 500 to 600 calories and 30 grams of fat?!

BITE IT! Get your chocolate fix with a hot cocoa. Even if it is made with whole milk, you'll save more than 300 calories and 20 grams of fat!

Nutritional information based on averages.

sweet 'n cinn-ful pretzel

PER SERVING (1 pretzel): 175 calories, 2g fat, 450mg sodium, 36g carbs, 1g fiber, 1g sugars, 5g protein

✴ Ingredients

1 plain frozen soft pretzel (about 2 ounces)
1 tablespoon Splenda No Calorie Sweetener (granulated)
⅛ teaspoon cinnamon
⅛ teaspoon salt
10 sprays I Can't Believe It's Not Butter! Spray

✴ Directions

Preheat oven to 400 degrees.

In a small bowl, mix Splenda, cinnamon, and salt. Set aside.

Spray a small baking pan lightly with nonstick spray. Place pretzel in pan and bake for 2 minutes.

Remove pretzel and spray each side evenly with butter spray (5 sprays per side). Next, cover entire pretzel with Splenda/cinnamon/salt mixture.

Bake for an additional 6 minutes, flipping halfway through. Enjoy!

MAKES 1 SERVING

HG SHOCKER!
Slip up and order a sweet 'n buttery pretzel from the mall food court and you could end up taking in as much as 400 calories and 10 grams of fat!

ginormous creamy frozen caramel crunchcake

PER SERVING (entire recipe): 130 calories, 0.5g fat, 70mg sodium, 28g carbs, 0g fiber, 8g sugars, 2g protein

✶✶ *This dessert is soooo great because it's huuuuge, crunchy, and very fun to eat!* ✶✶

✶ Ingredients

2 full-sized caramel corn rice cakes
¼ cup Cool Whip Free

✶ Directions

Cover the top half of one rice cake evenly with the Cool Whip. Gently place the other rice cake on top, making a sandwich. Freeze for at least 1 hour, then enjoy.

MAKES 1 SERVING

***HG Tip:** For an extra layer of fun, spread a tablespoon of fruity sugar-free preserves on the inside of each rice cake before assembling your treat. (Pssst . . . strawberry is the best!) It'll only add about 20 calories!*

berry-licious cupcakes

This recipe was co-developed with Weight Watchers®.

✶ Ingredients

For Frosting

One-half 8-ounce container Cool Whip Free

¼ cup fat-free cream cheese, softened

2 tablespoons Splenda No Calorie Sweetener (granulated)

½ tablespoon zero-calorie sugar-free strawberry syrup

⅛ teaspoon vanilla extract

1 drop neon pink food coloring

For Cupcakes

2 cups moist-style white cake mix (½ of an 18.25-ounce box)

1 cup diet black cherry soda

½ cup egg whites (about 4 egg whites)

6 medium strawberries, pureed

✶ Directions

Preheat oven to 350 degrees.

Combine all frosting ingredients in a medium bowl. Using an electric mixer at medium-low speed, blend for about 1 minute (until frosting is thoroughly mixed). Chill frosting in the freezer for 20 minutes and then transfer to the fridge (until ready to frost cupcakes).

In a large bowl, stir to combine cake mix, soda and egg whites. Add pureed strawberries and food coloring, and mix with electric mixer at medium-high speed until smooth (about 45 seconds). Evenly spoon batter into a 12-cup muffin pan spritzed with nonstick cooking spray or lined with baking cups.

Place pan in the oven and bake 15 to 20 minutes (until firm). Let cool completely before frosting. Once cool, remove cupcakes from the pan and evenly spread frosting over them.

MAKES 12 SERVINGS

Would You Rather . . .

So you saved room for dessert at your favorite restaurant. And you've been eyeing the tiramisu since you walked in the door. Before you order, know that it's likely to cost you at least 930 calories and 60 grams of fat. Hope you set some time aside to burn all those calories. Here's what you'll need to do to work 'em off:

✳ Climb stairs nonstop for more than 2½ hours *or*

✳ Rearrange the heaviest furniture in your house for about 3 hours straight *or*

✳ Scrub the kitchen floor for almost 4 hours!

Times based on estimates for a 150-pound woman.

chapter eleven

zappuccino

coffee shop swaps

blend for yourself. smoothies and shakes in your kitchen.

This chapter contains some of the BEST and most fun recipes in the book. One of the HG rules (and there aren't many!) is that you should, in general, avoid drinking tons of calories. Chewing and swallowing food is more satisfying than sipping stuff through a straw. But that doesn't mean you have to write off decadent drinks. The key is to find that balance—stick with shakes and smoothies that taste great yet top out at about 200 calories or less (especially if they're just snacks!). You'll find plenty of those right here. Some of the recipes actually beat out high-calorie versions in side-by-side taste tests (this is 100 percent true). Try 'em out and see for yourself!

vanillalicious cafe freeze

PER SERVING (entire recipe): 103 calories, 1g fat, 117mg sodium, 17g carbs, 0g fiber, 9g sugars, 4g protein

✳✳ *My secret weapon for making blended coffee swaps taste creamy (without adding lots of fat and calories) is DEFINITELY Coffee-mate Fat Free French Vanilla powdered creamer. That stuff is amazing—and a little goes a loooong way. Even a teaspoon or two (which has just about 13 to 25 calories) can make your drink CRAZY-creamy!* ✳✳

✶ Ingredients

5 ounces light vanilla soymilk

1 ounce sugar-free calorie-free vanilla syrup

1 tablespoon Coffee-mate Fat Free French Vanilla powdered creamer, dissolved in 1 ounce warm water

1 teaspoon instant coffee

3 no-calorie sweetener packets

5 to 8 ice cubes *or* 1 cup crushed ice

2 tablespoons Fat Free Reddi-wip

✶ Directions

Place all of the ingredients in a blender, except for the Reddi-wip. Blend on high speed for 30 to 45 seconds, until thoroughly blended. Pour into a tall glass and then finish off with whipped topping. It's a vanilla dream!

MAKES 1 SERVING

HG SHOCKER!

A large blended vanilla coffee drink with whipped cream contains an average of 540 calories and more than 15 grams of fat!

mint mocha freeze

PER SERVING (entire recipe): 55 calories, <0.5g fat, 37mg sodium, 13g carbs, 0g fiber, 4g sugars, 0g protein

✴ Ingredients

1 ounce sugar-free calorie-free peppermint syrup

1 tablespoon sugar-free chocolate syrup

2 teaspoons Coffee-mate Fat Free French Vanilla powdered creamer, dissolved in 1 ounce warm water

1 teaspoon instant coffee

3 no-calorie sweetener packets

5 to 8 ice cubes *or* 1 cup crushed ice

2 tablespoons Fat Free Reddi-wip

✴ Directions

Place all of the ingredients in a blender, except for the Reddi-wip. Add 6 ounces of water. Blend on high speed for 30 to 45 seconds, until completely blended. Pour into a tall glass and top with whipped topping. Enjoy your magical, minty-licious frozen treat!

MAKES 1 SERVING

strawberry cloud

✳✳ *This blended beverage is so good that it actually beat out Starbucks' version in a blind taste test. Try it!!!* ✳✳

✳ Ingredients

⅔ cup frozen strawberries

5 ounces light vanilla soymilk

2 teaspoons Coffee-mate Fat Free French Vanilla powdered creamer, dissolved in 1 ounce warm water

1 ounce sugar-free calorie-free strawberry syrup

3 no-calorie sweetener packets

3 to 4 ice cubes *or* ½ cup crushed ice

2 tablespoons Fat Free Reddi-wip

✳ Directions

Place all of the ingredients in a blender, except for the whipped topping. Blend on high speed for 30 to 45 seconds (until mixed thoroughly). Pour into a tall glass and top with Reddi-wip. Strawberrylicious!

MAKES 1 SERVING

HG SHOCKER!

Sure, a strawberry shake SOUNDS like it would be a healthy treat, but an average one contains about 650 calories and 20+ grams of fat. Berry scary!

peanut butter cup milkshake

PER SERVING (entire recipe): 188 calories, 6.5g fat, 324mg sodium, 29g carbs, 2g fiber, 9g sugars, 7g protein

✶ Ingredients

½ cup light chocolate soymilk
1 Jell-O Sugar Free Chocolate Pudding Snack
2 teaspoons reduced-fat peanut butter
3 no-calorie sweetener packets
5 to 8 ice cubes *or* 1 cup crushed ice
Optional: Fat Free Reddi-wip

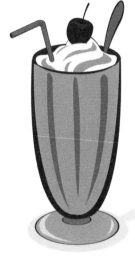

✶ Directions

Place all ingredients in a blender and blend at high speed for 45 to 60 seconds (until smooth). Pour into a tall glass and enjoy!

MAKES 1 SERVING

For Weight Watchers *POINTS*®
values and photos of all the
recipes in this book, check out
hungry-girl.com/book.

banana cream pie bonanza

PER SERVING (entire recipe): 168 calories, 1.5g fat, 132mg sodium, 34g carbs, 2g fiber, 20g sugars, 6g protein

✴✴ *This frozen dessert drink (or breakfast smoothie) tastes exactly like a banana cream pie . . . except frozen and through a straw. Yum!* ✴✴

✴ Ingredients

⅓ cup light vanilla soymilk

2 ounces fat-free vanilla yogurt

½ medium banana, sliced and frozen

3 no-calorie sweetener packets

1 teaspoon Coffee-mate Fat Free French Vanilla powdered creamer, dissolved in 1 ounce warm water

5 to 8 ice cubes *or* 1 cup crushed ice

½ sheet (2 crackers) low-fat honey graham crackers, crushed

2 tablespoons Fat Free Reddi-wip

✴ Directions

Place soymilk, yogurt, banana slices, sweetener, creamer mixture, and ice in the blender. Add 2 ounces of water. Blend on the highest speed for 30 to 45 seconds (until completely blended). Then stir in half of the crushed graham crackers.

Pour into a tall, pretty glass. Top with whipped topping. Sprinkle remaining graham cracker pieces on top. Enjoy!

MAKES 1 SERVING

TOP ATE Ways to Zazzle Up Your Guilt-Free Blended Beverages!
Stock your kitchen with these and your blended bevs will thank you . . .

1. Sugar-Free Flavored Syrups (1 ounce = 0 calories, 0g fat)

2. Splenda Flavors for Coffee (1 packet = 0 calories, 0g fat)

3. Fat-Free Flavored Powdered Non-Dairy Creamer (1 teaspoon = 13 calories, 0g fat)

4. Fat-Free Whipped Topping (2 tablespoons = 5 to 15 calories, 0g fat)

5. Frozen Fruit (½ cup = 35 calories, <0.5g fat)

6. Light Vanilla Soymilk (4 ounces = 35 calories, 1g fat)

7. Sugar-Free Powdered Drink Mixes (1 serving = 5 calories, 0g fat)

8. Tall Pretty Glasses with Cute Straws (no calories and no fat!!!)

Nutritional information based on averages.

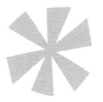

creamy orange dreamfloat

PER SERVING (entire recipe): 60 calories, 1g fat, 150mg sodium, 12g carbs, 0g fiber, 4g sugars, 0g protein

✷✷ *Frozen Cool Whip Free is a fantastic low-calorie swap for ice cream! Try this out with diet root beer, too!* ✷✷

✶ Ingredients

½ cup Cool Whip Free, frozen
1 can diet orange soda
1 flexy straw

✶ Directions

Pour soda into a glass. Top off glass with ½ scoop of the Cool Whip. Insert straw and enjoy!

MAKES 1 SERVING

HG Tip: About an hour before preparing this drink, put a glass mug in the freezer for a frosty float!

cookie-rific ice cream freeze

PER SERVING (entire recipe): 160 calories, 2.5g fat, 189mg sodium, 28g carbs, 1.5g fiber, 14g sugars, 6g protein

✳✳ *This is sooooo much like an Oreo McFlurry from McDonald's, but it has a tiny fraction of the calories!* ✳✳

✳ Ingredients

5 ounces light vanilla soymilk

¼ cup fat-free vanilla ice cream

½ pack of 100 Calorie Packs Oreo Thin Crisps *or* ¾ sheet (3 crackers) chocolate graham crackers

1 teaspoon Coffee-mate Fat Free French Vanilla powdered creamer, dissolved in 1 ounce warm water

2 no-calorie sweetener packets

5 to 8 ice cubes *or* 1 cup crushed ice

Optional: Fat Free Reddi-wip

✳ Directions

Place all ingredients in blender. Blend on high for 45 to 60 seconds (until mixed thoroughly). Pour into a tall glass and enjoy. Mmmmmm!

MAKES 1 SERVING

 For a pic of this recipe, see the photo insert. Yay!

HG SHOCKER!

The average cookies and cream shake packs in a ridiculous 900 calories and 55 grams of fat. How embarrassing!

super-duper cocoa-rific coffee malt

PER SERVING (entire recipe): 69 calories, 1g fat, 62mg sodium, 11g carbs, 0.5g fiber, 4g sugars, 2g protein

✶✶ *This is one of my most popular coffee treats. It's so easy to make (no blender required) and it's really decadent and fun. The cocoa and the malted milk powder taste especially great together. It's hard to believe this huge, creamy, sweet drink has less than 70 calories!* ✶✶

✶ Ingredients

¼ cup light vanilla soymilk

1 tablespoon fat-free non-dairy liquid creamer

2 teaspoons malted milk powder

1 teaspoon unsweetened cocoa powder

1 teaspoon instant coffee

3 no-calorie sweetener packets

5 to 8 ice cubes *or* 1 cup crushed ice

✶ Directions

Put all dry ingredients in a tall glass. Add 2 ounces of hot water and stir until ingredients have completely dissolved. Add ice and 5 ounces of cold water. Top off with soymilk and creamer, and give it a stir. AWESOME!

MAKES 1 SERVING

For Weight Watchers *POINTS*® values and photos of all the recipes in this book, check out hungry-girl.com/book.

CHEW ON THIS:

Americans spend about $10 billion annually at coffee outlets, according to the Specialty Coffee Association of America.

Would You Rather . . .

Oops! You ordered a large blended coffee frappé and slurped it down while running errands. That frozen faux pas cost you about 550 calories and 20 grams of fat! To burn that off you'd have to:

✳ Hand wash your car in the heat for nearly 3 hours *or*

✳ Grocery shop for 3 hours nonstop and then spend 45 minutes putting everything back 'cuz you forgot your wallet *or*

✳ Stand in line at the non-air-conditioned post office for about 6 hours!

Times based on estimates for a 150-pound woman.

chapter twelve

happy hour

cocktails

time to toss back some guilt-free sips.

Alcohol has lots of calories. That's not exactly a secret. The key to making guilt-free cocktails is figuring out what low-cal stuff to mix *with* that alcohol. That's where HG comes in! This chapter features some amazingly delicious drinks—and they each have no more than 175 calories (in fact, most have closer to 100). Keep in mind, any of these can be made without alcohol, and if you drink 'em that way (virgin style), you'll be saving close to 100 calories a drink. Cheers!

magical low-calorie margarita

PER SERVING (entire recipe): 115 calories, 0g fat, 55mg sodium, 2g carbs, 0g fiber, <0.5g sugars, 0g protein

✸✸ *This recipe is so awesome, you'll be able to fool everyone into thinking they're drinking a super-high-calorie margarita. If you don't like your drinks super-sweet, feel free to use just half of the lemonade drink mix.* ✸✸

✸ Ingredients

6 ounces diet lemon-lime soda

1½ ounces tequila

1 packet (two 5-calorie servings) sugar-free powdered lemonade drink mix

2 tablespoons lime juice

5 to 8 ice cubes *or* 1 cup crushed ice

Optional: lime wedge (for garnish)

✸ Directions

Stir all ingredients together, except for the ice.

For a frozen drink, place mixture in a blender with the ice and blend until smooth. Or simply pour mixture over ice and enjoy. If you like, serve with a lime wedge.

MAKES 1 SERVING

 For a pic of this recipe, see the photo insert.

chilly chocolate mudslide

PER SERVING (entire recipe): 158 calories, 0.5g fat, 185mg sodium, 11g carbs, 1g fiber, 7g sugars, 3g protein

✶ Ingredients

One 25-calorie packet diet hot cocoa mix
¼ cup light chocolate soymilk
1½ ounces vodka
½ ounce sugar-free calorie-free syrup (white chocolate or vanilla)
1 teaspoon sugar-free chocolate syrup
2 no-calorie sweetener packets
5 to 8 ice cubes *or* 1 cup crushed ice
Optional: Fat Free Reddi-wip

✶ Directions

Dissolve cocoa mix and sweetener into 3 ounces of hot water. Add soymilk, vodka, and both syrups. Stir well.

Place mixture in a blender with the ice and blend on high speed for about 45 seconds (until thoroughly blended).

Pour and, if you like, top off with a squirt of whipped topping!

MAKES 1 SERVING

piña colada freeze

PER SERVING (entire recipe): 156 calories, <0.5g fat, 41mg sodium, 18g carbs, 0.5g fiber, 12g sugars, 2g protein

✳✳ *This is definitely the most decadent of all . . . and definitely one of the best piña coladas you'll ever have. It's extremely creamy but NOT sickeningly sweet!* ✳✳

✳ Ingredients

1½ ounces coconut rum

1½ ounces sugar-free calorie-free coconut syrup

¼ cup fat-free vanilla ice cream

1 tablespoon canned crushed pineapple in juice

1 no-calorie sweetener packet

5 to 8 ice cubes *or* 1 cup crushed ice

✳ Directions

Place all ingredients in a blender. Blend on high speed for about 30 seconds (until mixture is smooth and completely blended).

Pour and enjoy!

MAKES 1 SERVING

📷 For a pic of this recipe, see the photo insert. Yay!

Cocktail Mixer Face-Off!

Check out all the calories you can save . . .

Sip It	Skip It
Sugar-Free Fruity Syrups—0 Calories	Full-Sugar Syrups—70 calories
Light Vanilla Soymilk—9 calories	Sour Mix—30 calories
Sugar-Free Fruit Drink Mixes—1 calorie	Tonic Water—10 calories
Club Soda—0 calories	Heavy Cream—100 calories (and 10g fat!)
Diet Lemon-Lime Soda—0 Calories	Fruit Juices—17 calories

Nutritional information based on averages for 1-ounce servings.

Would You Rather . . .

You finally took that vacation and decided to take advantage of the happy-hour drink special. That creamy frozen piña colada will cost you about 650 calories and 20 grams of fat! To burn all of that off you would have to:

✱ Battle seaweed and jellyfish in the ocean nonstop for nearly 1½ hours *or*

✱ Face off solo against the tennis ball machine (set at warp speed!) for almost 2 hours *or*

✱ Trudge barefoot across the hot sand for more than 3 hours!

Times based on estimates for a 150-pound woman.

3-for-1 special cherry vodkatini

PER SERVING (⅓rd of recipe): 97 calories, 0g fat, 5mg sodium, 0g carbs, 0g fiber, 0g sugars, 0g protein

✶ Ingredients

4½ ounces vodka
½ packet (one 5-calorie serving) sugar-free powdered cherry drink mix
3 ounces diet cherry lemon-lime soda or diet black cherry soda
8 to 10 ice cubes

✶ Directions

Dissolve the drink mix into 6 ounces of cold water. Stir thoroughly.

Combine mixture with vodka and ice, put it in a shaker (or some other glass with a lid), cover tightly, and shake well.

Strain drink evenly into 3 martini glasses. Top each glass with an ounce of the soda.

MAKES 3 SERVINGS

CHEW ON THIS:

The term "toast," meaning a wish for good health, originated in ancient Rome, where an actual piece of toasted bread was dropped into wine.

kickin' cranberry cosmo

PER SERVING (entire recipe): 100 calories, 0g fat, 32mg sodium, 2g carbs, 0g fiber, 1g sugars, 0g protein

✳ Ingredients

5 ounces Diet Ocean Spray Cranberry Spray juice drink
1½ ounces vodka
1 teaspoon lime juice
5 to 8 ice cubes
Optional: splash of diet lemon-lime soda, lime wedge (for garnish)

✳ Directions

Combine vodka, cranberry juice drink, and lime juice. Stir thoroughly.

Combine mixture with ice, put it in a shaker (or some other glass with a lid), cover tightly, and shake well.

Strain drink into a large martini glass.

If you like, top with a splash of soda and garnish with a lime wedge. Enjoy!

MAKES 1 SERVING

mojito madness

✷✷ Mojitos ROCK! This recipe is sooo simple and sooo good. ✷✷

✷ Ingredients

6 ounces diet lemon-lime soda

12 mint leaves

¼ lime, cut into slices

1½ ounces rum

5 to 8 ice cubes

Optional: additional mint leaves and lime wedges (for garnish)

✷ Directions

Muddle (aka pulverize) the mint and lime in a glass.

Add the soda and rum, stir well.

Add ice and enjoy! Feel free to garnish with mint and lime.

MAKES 1 SERVING

wicked good white russian

✶ Ingredients

1½ ounces vodka

1½ ounces light vanilla soymilk

2 teaspoons sugar-free calorie-free vanilla syrup

2 teaspoons Coffee-mate Fat Free French Vanilla powdered creamer

1 teaspoon instant coffee

4 to 6 ice cubes

✶ Directions

Dissolve creamer and coffee in ¼ cup of warm water.

Add soymilk and syrup. Stir well.

Add vodka and ice. Stir and enjoy.

MAKES 1 SERVING

slammin' slimmed-down strawberry daiquiri

PER SERVING (entire recipe): 121 calories, 0g fat, 10mg sodium, 4g carbs, 0.5g fiber, 2g sugars, 0g protein

✶✶ *Drink mix blends like strawberry kiwi, strawberry banana, and tangerine strawberry make the most awesome strawberry daiquiris EVER! And even though strawberry is the most famous and popular flavor for daiquiris, why stop there? There are so many great flavors of sugar-free drink mixes, your options are almost limitless . . . Have fun!* ✶✶

✶ Ingredients

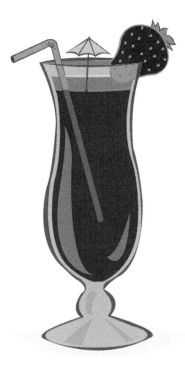

1½ ounces rum

1 packet (two 5-calorie servings) sugar-free powdered drink mix (any strawberry blend)

3 frozen strawberries

1 tablespoon lime juice

5 to 8 ice cubes *or* 1 cup crushed ice

✶ Directions

Dissolve drink mix into 4 ounces of water. Stir thoroughly.

In a blender, combine drink mixture with all other ingredients. Blend to desired consistency.

Pour, add a straw, and slurp that baby up!

MAKES 1 SERVING

TOP ATE Shockingly High-Cal Alcoholic Drinks

See what the bartender is really serving up . . .

1. Piña Colada—Think twice about downing this 650-calorie drink while wearing a bathing suit. Yikes!

2. White Russian—This creamy drink has 425 fatty calories.

3. Mudslide—This 850-calorie so-called chocolate "dream" actually gives us nightmares.

4. Champagne Cocktail—Why spend 250 calories on this when a glass of champagne has just 100?

5. Frozen Margarita—A 740-calorie glass of lime-flavored slush?! Ay caramba!

6. Daiquiri—This one clocks in at 675 calories. Um, no thanks.

7. Mai Tai—350 calories . . . a total waste, and way too sweet.

8. Long Island Iced Tea—The average LIT packs in 780 calories. OMG!

Nutritional information based on averages for typical serving sizes of each drink.

CHEW ON THIS:

Alcohol increases insulin production in the body, which can increase your appetite. No worries! Just whip up some HG snack recipes in advance and you'll have low-calorie things to chew on when the mood hits you!

chapter thirteen

fun with . . .

recipes featuring hg favorites

tofu shirataki noodles, canned pumpkin, and butternut squash

This chapter is all about having a little fun with some special ingredients. Canned pumpkin, butternut squash, and Tofu Shirataki noodles are all HG staples because they taste great, are good for you, and are crazy-low in calories. We recommend keeping a few cans of pumpkin in the kitchen cabinet, a few bags of Tofu Shirataki in the fridge, and several butternut squash in the basement. Then you'll always have the key ingredients on hand for the fantastic recipes here. From pancakes and puddings to home fries and fettuccine Alfredo—it's all here!

fun with tofu shirataki noodles

House Foods Tofu Shirataki is a dieter's dream. Pasta is a food that so many people think they simply CANNOT eat when they're counting calories. That's why these super-low-cal "noodles" (which are actually tofu-infused strands of yam flour) can be life-changing—literally! When I first discovered these, I started cooking with them like crazy, making all kinds of Alfredo dishes, stir-frys, spaghetti recipes, and more. The Tofu Shirataki recipes in this chapter are some HG favorites, but you'll find more recipes that call for these noodles throughout the book. By the way, if you have trouble locating House Foods Tofu Shirataki (at select supermarkets, natural foods stores, or Japanese markets) you can also try these recipes using regular shirataki noodles (the ones made without tofu). Those are not quite as pasta-like, but they aren't a bad Tofu Shirataki substitute.

fettuccine hungry girlfredo

PER SERVING (entire recipe): 81 calories, 3g fat, 242mg sodium, 9g carbs, 4g fiber, <1g sugars, 4g protein

✴ ✴ *This recipe may be the most popular Hungry Girl recipe EVER . . . and with good reason. It's really great! Feel free to add shrimp, chicken, steak, veggies—whatever—to it. This stuff is mind-blowingly fantastic! If you like your noodles super-cheesy, feel free to use the entire wedge of cheese. You'll only tack on about 17 calories to your dish.* ✴ ✴

✴ Ingredients

1 package House Foods Tofu Shirataki, Fettuccine Shape
½ wedge The Laughing Cow cheese, Light Original Swiss
2 teaspoons reduced-fat Parmesan-style grated topping
1 teaspoon fat-free sour cream
Optional: salt and black pepper

✴ Directions

Rinse and drain shirataki noodles well. Pat dry. Place noodles in a microwave-safe bowl and microwave for 1 minute.

Drain excess liquid from noodles and pat them until thoroughly dry. Slice noodles up a bit for fettuccine-length pieces.

Add cheese, grated topping, and sour cream. Mix well. Microwave for 1 minute and then stir.

If you like, add salt and black pepper to taste.

MAKES 1 SERVING

rockin' tuna noodle casserole

PER SERVING (¼th of casserole): 167 calories, 5g fat, 894mg sodium, 14g carbs, 4g fiber, 2g sugars, 17g protein

✳ Ingredients

3 packages House Foods Tofu Shirataki, Fettuccine Shape
7 ounces canned tuna (packed in water), drained and flaked
One 10.75-ounce can Campbell's 98% Fat Free Cream of Mushroom Soup
1 wedge The Laughing Cow Light Original Swiss cheese
½ cup frozen peas
3 tablespoons reduced-fat Parmesan-style grated topping, divided
Salt, black pepper, and garlic powder, to taste
Optional: cayenne pepper

✳ Directions

Preheat oven to 375 degrees.

Rinse and drain shirataki noodles well. Pat dry. Place noodles in a microwave-safe bowl and microwave for 1 minute.

Drain excess liquid from noodles and pat them until thoroughly dry. Slice noodles up a bit for fettuccine-length pieces.

Add cheese wedge to noodles and microwave for an additional 20 seconds. Mix well.

Add tuna, peas, soup, and just 1 tablespoon of the grated topping. Mix well.

Season to taste with salt, black pepper, and garlic powder. For an extra kick, add cayenne pepper, if desired.

Evenly top dish with the remaining 2 tablespoons of grated topping. Bake dish in the oven for 20 to 25 minutes (until hot and bubbly).

MAKES 4 SERVINGS

noodled-up zucchini pancakes

PER SERVING (1 pancake): 50 calories, 0.5g fat, 295mg sodium, 9g carbs, 1g fiber, 2g sugars, 3g protein

✳ Ingredients

2 packages House Foods Tofu Shirataki, Spaghetti Shape
4½ cups shredded or grated zucchini
1 cup dry pancake mix
1 cup diced mushrooms
¾ cup chopped scallions
½ cup egg whites (about 4 egg whites)
1 teaspoon salt

✳ Directions

Rinse and drain noodles well. Pat dry. Place noodles in a microwave-safe bowl and microwave for 1 minute.

Drain excess liquid from noodles and pat them until thoroughly dry. Cut noodles into pieces (about 3 inches long). Set aside.

Combine egg whites, pancake mix, and salt in a bowl. Stir in noodles, scallions, mushrooms, and zucchini. Mix well.

Spray a pan with nonstick spray and set over medium heat.

Evenly place three ⅓-cup scoops of the mixture in the pan, and use a spatula to flatten into pancakes. Cook until both sides of each pancake are golden brown, flipping occasionally. Repeat this process 4 more times, removing pan from heat and respraying each time and stirring remaining mixture in between batches.

MAKES 15 SERVINGS

 For a pic of this recipe, see the photo insert. Yay!

• •

TOP ATE Things to Know About Tofu Shirataki
The noodle-y need-to-know info . . .

1. They can be found in the refrigerated section of the market, near the tofu.

2. They come floating in a bag of water. Do not be put off by this.

3. You should rinse them very well before using.

4. Once rinsed, dry thoroughly by blotting them with paper towels repeatedly, or even stir-frying 'em over medium heat to get rid of excess water. This step is super-important!

5. You don't need to cook them at all. Just nuke 'em in the microwave for a minute and they're ready to use.

6. They're CRAZY-long and unwieldy. They should be cut, no matter how you prepare them.

7. The texture of these noodles is a little more chewy and slippery than regular pasta. Just a heads-up.

8. Tofu Shirataki works best with thick, creamy sauces. The Laughing Cow Light cheese wedges work especially well as a sauce ingredient.

---

super-duper spaghetti pie

PER SERVING (¼th of pie): 83 calories, 1.5g fat, 588mg sodium, 8g carbs, 2g fiber, 4g sugars, 10g protein

✳ Ingredients

1 package House Foods Tofu Shirataki, Spaghetti Shape
1 cup canned tomato sauce, divided
1 cup assorted sliced veggies (onions, peppers, mushrooms, etc.)
½ cup fat-free liquid egg substitute
⅓ cup shredded fat-free mozzarella cheese
15 pieces (about 1 ounce) turkey pepperoni

✳ Directions

Preheat oven to 425 degrees.

Rinse and drain shirataki noodles well. Pat dry. Place noodles in a microwave-safe bowl and microwave for 1 minute.

Drain excess liquid from noodles and pat them until thoroughly dry. Cut noodles up a bit for spaghetti-length pieces.

In a round baking dish, combine noodles, veggies, egg substitute, and ¾ cup tomato sauce. Mix well.

Bake for about 25 minutes or until firm.

Remove pie from the oven and spread remaining ¼ cup of tomato sauce over it. Place turkey pepperoni on top and then sprinkle evenly with cheese.

Return pie to the oven until the cheese has melted. Allow to cool a bit (if you can!) and enjoy.

MAKES 4 SERVINGS

sweet cheese 'n peach cinnamon raisin kugel

PER SERVING (¼th of kugel): 75 calories, 0.5g fat, 202mg sodium, 11g carbs, 2g fiber, 7g sugars, 6g protein

✶ Ingredients

1 package House Foods Tofu Shirataki, Fettuccine Shape
1 large firm peach, cut into bite-sized pieces
¼ cup fat-free liquid egg substitute
¼ cup fat-free cream cheese, softened
¼ cup fat-free cottage cheese
2 tablespoons raisins
2 tablespoons Splenda No Calorie Sweetener (granulated)
¼ teaspoon vanilla extract
¼ teaspoon cinnamon
dash salt

✶ Directions

Preheat oven to 425 degrees.

Combine egg substitute, cream cheese, Splenda, vanilla extract, cinnamon, and salt. Stir until completely blended and free of lumps. Mix in cottage cheese and raisins, and then set aside.

Rinse and drain shirataki noodles well. Pat dry. Slice noodles into small pieces.

Over medium heat, toss noodles in a pan until they are thoroughly dry and beginning to toughen (about 1 minute). Transfer noodles to a mixing bowl, and top with the peaches.

Combine cheese mixture with the noodles and peaches, and stir well. Transfer it all to a medium-small baking dish sprayed with nonstick spray.

Place dish in the oven, and bake for 25 - 30 minutes, or until firm. Enjoy!

MAKES 4 SERVINGS

crazy-good cold sesame noodles

PER SERVING (entire recipe): 198 calories, 10g fat, 494mg sodium, 19g carbs, 6g fiber, 4g sugars, 9g protein

✷✷ *These noodles are soooo good! Once you taste 'em, you'll probably never ever eat regular cold sesame noodles again. Good riddance!* ✷✷

✷ Ingredients

1 package House Foods Tofu Shirataki, Spaghetti Shape
1 tablespoon plus 1 teaspoon reduced-fat peanut butter, at room temperature
1 ounce light soymilk
2 tablespoons chopped scallions
½ tablespoon light or low-sodium soy sauce
½ teaspoon sesame seeds
⅛ teaspoon minced garlic
1 no-calorie sweetener packet
Optional: salt

✷ Directions

Rinse and drain noodles well. Pat dry. Place noodles in a microwave-safe bowl and microwave for 1 minute.

Drain excess liquid from noodles and pat them until thoroughly dry. Cut noodles into spaghetti-length pieces. Set aside.

In a small dish, combine peanut butter, soymilk, soy sauce, sesame seeds, garlic, and sweetener. Mix well. Feel free to season this sauce, to taste, with salt.

Pour sauce over noodles. Mix thoroughly. Top with chopped scallions and mix again.

Allow to chill in the fridge. Then enjoy!

MAKES 1 SERVING

 For a pic of this recipe, see the photo insert. Yay!

noodlicious veggie crabcakes

PER SERVING (1 crabcake): 60 calories, 0.5g fat, 326mg sodium, 10g carbs, 1g fiber, 2g sugars, 5g protein

✳✳ *These veggie-packed crabcakes are definitely not like any crabcakes you've ever had before. They're so good with some fat-free sour cream, and they taste great dipped in Dijonnaise, too!* ✳✳

✳ Ingredients

2 packages House Foods Tofu Shirataki, Spaghetti Shape

One 12-ounce package broccoli cole slaw mix, dry

1½ cups dry pancake mix

12 ounces drained white crabmeat

1 cup diced scallions

½ cup egg whites (about 4 egg whites)

1 teaspoon seasoned salt

Salt and black pepper, to taste

✳ Directions

Rinse and drain shirataki noodles well. Pat dry. Place noodles in a microwave-safe bowl and microwave for 1 minute.

Drain excess liquid from noodles and pat them until thoroughly dry. Cut noodles into pieces about 4 inches in length.

Combine all ingredients and mix well. Bring a pan sprayed with nonstick spray to medium heat.

Evenly scoop 4 spoonfuls into pan (using a total of one-fifth of the batter). Press gently with a spatula to form cakes. Cook until crabcakes are golden brown on both sides, flipping occasionally. Repeat this process 4 more times, removing the pan from the heat and respraying it in between batches.

MAKES 20 SERVINGS

For Weight Watchers *POINTS*® values and photos of all the recipes in this book, check out hungry-girl.com/book.

fun with canned pumpkin

Canned pumpkin is magical. Over the past few years, its popularity has grown so much that markets often find themselves running out of the stuff. Keep cans of it in the pantry at all times—running out of it is no fun! Pumpkin is super-low in calories (40 per ½ cup), has practically no fat, and is loaded with fiber (3.5 grams per serving). Use it in soups, sauces, for baking, in oatmeal—wherever. Pumpkin ROCKS. There are recipes that call for pumpkin throughout this book, but here are some pumpkin-y HG favorites . . .

pumpkin crunchers

PER SERVING (1 piece): 39 calories, <0.5g fat, 49mg sodium, 10g carbs, 2g fiber, 2g sugars, 1g protein

✶✶ *This is a fun little pumpkin dessert. The crunchers taste best when eaten within a day or so (after that, they get a little too hard and need to be slightly thawed before eating).* ✶✶

✶ Ingredients

One-half 15-ounce can pure pumpkin
One-half 8-ounce container Cool Whip Free
2 Jell-O Sugar Free Vanilla Pudding Snacks
¾ cup Fiber One bran cereal (original)
Cinnamon, to taste

✶ Directions

Combine pumpkin, Cool Whip, and pudding in a bowl. Mix well.

Season mixture to taste with cinnamon. Stir in Fiber One.

Spoon batter evenly into a 12-cup muffin pan (sprayed with nonstick spray or lined with baking cups).

Place pan in the freezer until crunchers are frozen.

MAKES 12 SERVINGS

creamy banana pumpkin pie pancakes

PER SERVING (3 pancakes): 243 calories, 2.5g fat, 451mg sodium, 39g carbs, 4.5g fiber, 9g sugars, 15g protein

✷✷ *Pssst . . . we like these drizzled with sugar-free maple syrup!* ✷✷

✶ Ingredients

⅓ cup regular oats (not instant)
1 tablespoon dry pancake mix
⅓ medium banana, mashed well with a fork
2 tablespoons pure pumpkin
⅓ cup fat-free liquid egg substitute
1 tablespoon fat-free cottage cheese
2 no-calorie sweetener packets
½ teaspoon pumpkin pie spice
¼ teaspoon vanilla extract
Dash of salt

✶ Directions

Combine all ingredients in a bowl with 3 tablespoons of water. Stir until thoroughly mixed.

In a pan sprayed with nonstick spray, over medium heat, drop batter into pan to form 3 pancakes. Once pancakes begin to look solid (about 3 minutes), gently flip.

Cook for about 3 more minutes or until both sides are lightly browned and insides are cooked through.

MAKES 1 SERVING

· ·

CHEW ON THIS:

Pumpkin is a great substitute for oil, butter, and other fatty ingredients used in baking.

upside-down pumpkin cheesecake

PER SERVING (1/10th of recipe): 121 calories, 1g fat, 204mg sodium, 23g carbs, 1.5g fiber, 6g sugars, 5g protein

✴✴ *This recipe was inspired by a Hungry Girl subscriber named Suzanne. Thanks, Suz!* ✴✴

✴ Ingredients

One 15-ounce can pure pumpkin
One 8-ounce container Cool Whip Free
One 8-ounce container fat-free cream cheese, at room temperature
⅞ cup fat-free sour cream (almost 1 cup but not quite)
3½ sheets (14 crackers) low-fat honey graham crackers, crushed
¾ cup to 1 cup Splenda No Calorie Sweetener (granulated)
1 tablespoon lemon juice
2 teaspoons pumpkin pie spice

✴ Directions

Combine cream cheese, Cool Whip, sour cream, lemon juice, and Splenda (adjust Splenda amount based on how sweet you like your cheesecake). Stir until thoroughly blended.

Add pumpkin and pumpkin pie spice. Mix well.

Spoon mixture evenly into a wide serving bowl. Top with crushed graham crackers.

Chill in the fridge for a few hours, then enjoy. Mmmmmmmm . . . pumpkinlicious!

MAKES 10 SERVINGS

wayne's pumpkin smash

PER SERVING (1 piece): 65 calories, <0.5g fat, 81mg sodium, 12g carbs, 1g fiber, 7g sugars, 5g protein

✷✷ *Wayne is an HG subscriber and our pal. He's also a writer for* The Tonight Show. *Now that we know Wayne, we not only get to eat AWESOME Pumpkin Smash but we get VIP seats to see Jay Leno!* ✷✷

✶ Ingredients

One 15-ounce can pure pumpkin
One 12-ounce can evaporated fat-free milk
½ cup fat-free liquid egg substitute
¾ cup Splenda No Calorie Sweetener (granulated)
2 teaspoons pumpkin pie spice

✶ Directions

Preheat oven to 350 degrees.

Combine all ingredients. Mix well.

Place mixture in a baking dish and bake in the oven for 45 minutes.

Once ready to serve (it's delicious eaten hot or cold), cut into 9 pieces.

MAKES 9 SERVINGS

For Weight Watchers **POINTS**® values and photos of all the recipes in this book, check out hungry-girl.com/book.

mug 'o pumpkin crème

PER SERVING (entire recipe): 79 calories, 1.5g fat, 127mg sodium,
10g carbs, 1.5g fiber, 6g sugars, 6g protein

✴ Ingredients

7 ounces light vanilla soymilk
2 tablespoons canned pure pumpkin
¼ teaspoon cornstarch
¼ teaspoon pumpkin pie spice
¼ teaspoon vanilla extract
No-calorie sweetener, to taste

✴ Directions

Combine all ingredients, except the
sweetener, in a small pot. Stir well.
Bring to a boil, stirring constantly.

Once mixture begins to froth, continue
to boil for 1 minute. Remove from heat and pour into a mug.

Allow to cool slightly. Sweeten, to taste, with your no-calorie sweetener of
choice and enjoy.

MAKES 1 SERVING

fun with butternut squash

Butternut squash is the most underrated food EVER. Not only is it amazingly delicious but it's also healthy, soooo low in calories, extremely versatile, and fun to cook. Granted, it is a little annoying to peel, cut, and deseed the things, but it's definitely worth the trouble. These recipes are so good, you may forget that sweet potatoes exist (b-nut squash tastes so similar, but has about half the calories!). And speaking of potatoes, don't miss HG's famous Bake-tastic Butternut Squash Fries on page 100. Happy squashing!

maplelicious
butternut squash mash

PER SERVING (½ of recipe): 109 calories, 1g fat, 341mg sodium,
27g carbs, 4g fiber, 5g sugars, 2g protein

✳ Ingredients

3 cups peeled and cubed butternut squash
2 tablespoons sugar-free maple syrup
1 teaspoon whipped light butter or light buttery spread
¼ teaspoon salt

✳ Directions

Place squash and ¼ cup of water in a
microwave-safe bowl and cover. Microwave
for 5 to 7 minutes, until soft.

Drain water from the bowl. Add syrup, butter,
and salt. Mash and stir. Enjoy!

MAKES 2 SERVINGS

squash-tastic shepherd's pie

PER SERVING (¼th of pie): 232 calories, 2.5g fat, 552mg sodium, 25g carbs, 4g fiber, 5g sugars, 28g protein

✸✸ *This shepherd's pie swap is AMAZING. My obsession with butternut squash really paid off here—in spades!* ✸✸

✸ Ingredients

1 pound raw extra-lean ground turkey

3½ cups peeled and cubed butternut squash

1½ cups frozen mixed vegetables

½ cup chopped onions

¾ cup fat-free gravy

1 tablespoon light whipped butter or light buttery spread

½ teaspoon minced garlic

¼ teaspoon salt

Dash of black pepper

Dash of garlic powder

Dash of onion powder

✸ Directions

Preheat oven to 400 degrees.

Place the squash in a large microwave-safe dish with ½ cup of water. Cover bowl and cook squash in the microwave for 12 to 14 minutes, until squash is soft.

Meanwhile, in a medium pan over medium heat, cook onions until slightly browned (2 to 3 minutes).

Add the turkey, minced garlic, garlic powder, onion powder, and black pepper to the pan. Stir well. Cook until meat is browned.

Drain any excess liquid from the pan. Place meat/onion mixture in a casserole dish. Pour gravy evenly over the mixture. Spread the mixed veggies on top and then set dish aside.

Once squash is cooked, drain excess water and mash well. Add butter and salt to the squash and then mix thoroughly. Layer the mashed squash on top of the veggie layer. Bake in the oven for 20 to 25 minutes (until crust looks slightly crispy).

MAKES 4 SERVINGS

📷 For a pic of this recipe, see the photo insert. Yay!

Butternut Squash Basics—Peeling & Cubing 101

Simple secrets for perfectly peeled 'n squared squash . . .

✳ Seek out a long squash with a short round section. The round part is tough to cube—it's mostly hollow, with seeds and fibers that need to be scraped and removed from the flesh. But the long part is all flesh, perfect for cubing.

✳ Start by hacking off the ends and then slicing the squash in half widthwise. Then you'll have 2 easy-to-work-with pieces with flat ends.

✳ Use a vegetable peeler to remove the skin. Drag it firmly down the length of the pieces in strips. Keep peeling until you get to the bright orangy-yellow part.

✳ Once your squash halves are peeled, use a sharp knife to cut them in half lengthwise. If squash is unusually firm and tough to slice, try nuking it in the microwave for 45 seconds to soften it.

✳ Carefully slice out the sections of the squash attached to the seeds and fibers and throw them away. Then chop the rest of the squash into evenly sized cubes.

✳ If you're still totally intimidated by the b-nut, scope out the produce section of the market for pre-cubed pieces. (We won't tell!)

yummy butternut home fries

PER SERVING (¼th of recipe): 58 calories, 2g fat, 63mg sodium, 11g carbs, 2g fiber, 3g sugars, 1g protein

✳ Ingredients

2 cups peeled and cubed butternut squash (1-inch cubes)
½ medium red bell pepper, chopped
½ medium onion, chopped
½ cup fat-free broth (chicken or vegetable)
½ tablespoon olive oil
¼ teaspoon pumpkin pie spice
Dash of cayenne pepper
Salt and black pepper, to taste

✳ Directions

Sauté onion with olive oil in a pan over low heat, until translucent (1 to 2 minutes).

Add bell pepper and continue to cook for 1 minute.

Add squash and stir. Turn heat up to medium and add salt, black pepper, pumpkin pie spice, and cayenne pepper. Mix well.

Cook for about 7 minutes, until squash starts to soften.

Raise heat to high and add broth. Bring to a boil. After 30 seconds of boiling, reduce heat to low.

Simmer until broth evaporates, stirring often.

Cover pan and continue to cook for 3 minutes or until squash is tender.

MAKES 4 SERVINGS

 For a pic of this recipe, see the photo insert. Yay!

. . . .

Health Benefits of Butternut Squash!
Three great reasons why we love our squashy orange friend . . .

✳ Butternut squash is an excellent source of vitamin A and a very good source of vitamin C, potassium, and fiber.

✳ This winter squash, dense in omega-3 fatty acids, is good for your heart and also your respiratory system.

✳ B-nut squash is also rich in vitamins B_1 and B_5, which help give you energy.

---

creamy butternut squash 'n apple breakfast treat

PER SERVING (½ of recipe): 102 calories, <0.5g fat, 321mg sodium, 26g carbs, 3.5g fiber, 10g sugars, 2g protein

✸✸ *Oh my! This recipe is soooooo delicious I can hardly stand it. Not sure if it qualifies as a hot cereal or not—but it is an AWESOME low-calorie breakfast!* ✸✸

✸ Ingredients

2 cups peeled and cubed butternut squash
½ cup chopped apples
1 ounce light vanilla soymilk
1 tablespoon sugar-free maple syrup
2 teaspoons brown sugar (not packed)
½ teaspoon pumpkin pie spice
¼ teaspoon salt
1 no-calorie sweetener packet
Optional: additional light vanilla soymilk

✸ Directions

Spray a small pot with nonstick spray and bring to medium-low heat.

Add squash and cook for 10 to 12 minutes, until squash is tender.

With a potato masher, mash squash in the pot. Add salt, pumpkin pie spice, and apple pieces. Mix well.

Turn heat to high and add 1 cup of water. Bring to a boil. After 30 seconds of boiling, reduce heat to low.

Let mixture simmer for about 3 minutes, until squash is tender and most of the water has evaporated, but apple still has some crunch to it.

Add maple syrup, brown sugar, sweetener, and soymilk. Mix thoroughly.

Continue to cook and stir until mixture reaches desired consistency (the longer you cook it, the thicker it will become).

If you like, top with an extra splash of soymilk before serving.

MAKES 2 SERVINGS

. . . .

Gettin' Picky With It
How to snap up the best butternut . . .

✳ Look for one that's firm and heavy for its size. And go for a dull surface rather than a shiny one.

✳ Avoid butternut squash that has a soft rind, is moldy, or has water-soaked areas (ewwww).

✳ The season for butternut squash (a winter squash) is August through March. Just know that you'll get the best picks between the months of October and November, because that is the peak season for winter squash.

creamy butternut squash & chipotle soup

✷ Ingredients

1 large butternut squash (big enough to yield 5 cups cubed)

4 cups fat-free chicken broth

2 cups chopped onions

2 whole chipotle peppers in adobo sauce (canned)

3 tablespoons fat-free liquid non-dairy creamer

¼ teaspoon ground cumin

Salt, to taste

✷ Directions

Preheat oven to 350 degrees.

Cut ends off of the squash. Slice squash in half lengthwise. Remove seeds and any additional fibers.

Place squash halves, flesh-side down, on a baking pan sprayed with nonstick spray. Cook in the oven for 25 minutes.

When the squash halves are cool enough to handle, peel them and cut into cubes. Measure out 5 cups and set aside.

In a large pot sprayed with nonstick spray, cook onions over medium heat for 5 minutes or until soft.

Add squash cubes, peppers, broth, and cumin. Reduce heat to low.

Allow mixture to simmer for 30 minutes or until squash is tender, stirring occasionally.

Remove from heat and allow to cool for several minutes.

Working in batches, place squash mixture in a blender and puree until smooth. Transfer pureed mixture to a large container.

Add creamer and mix thoroughly. Add salt to taste.

MAKES 5 SERVINGS

For Weight Watchers *POINTS*®
values and photos of all the
recipes in this book, check out
hungry-girl.com/book.

chapter fourteen

survival guides

survival of the fittest
taking on any and every eating-out option.

These mini survival guides will help you tackle food challenges—anytime, anywhere. No problem!

sushi survival 101

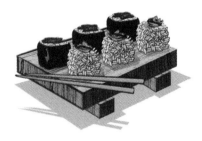

Get ready to sushi it up without swallowing boatloads of fatty stuff. HG's got the raw facts.

✳ At-a-Glance Glossary

Heads Up! Look out for the following words. They'll clue you in that you're about to order something not so diet-friendly . . .

Crunch—Just a cute and clever way of saying "fried and fatty."

Dynamite—In sushi-land, the word "dynamite" basically means "baked in a sea of gooey mayo." Skip it!

Spider—Spider rolls are usually greasy fried crab rolls. They may sound good, but they're packed with calories and fat.

Tempura—This is basically a Japanese version of battered, deep-fried food. Don't be fooled by low-calorie foods (like veggies and shrimp) in the form of tempura. Any tempura = a fatfest!

• •

Rockin' Rolls!

You can't go wrong with these restaurant regulars . . .

✳ **Cucumber Roll**—This crunchy, healthy delight packs in around 130 calories and nearly no fat!

✳ **Spicy Tuna Roll**—If made with a small amount of mayo, one of these will likely contain 250 to 290 calories and 5 to 10g of fat.

✳ **California Roll**—Order it without mayo and this one will set you back 270 to 300 calories, and have 5 to 10 grams of fat.

Nutritional information based on averages. One roll equals 6 large pieces or 8 small ones.

✶ Extra, Extra!

Items and ingredients to indulge in, and others to always avoid . . .

The Good—Soy sauce, rice vinegar, wasabi, ginger, seaweed, miso or clear soup, edamame, steamed dumplings.

The Not-So-Good—Oily or cream-based sauces, cream cheese, mayo, noodle or dumpling soup, tempura, fried dumplings.

- -

More Sushi Tips

✳ Grab a seat at the sushi bar. Not only will you be entertained but you'll find out firsthand exactly how much of each ingredient gets wrapped up in your rolls.

✳ Start your meal off with an appetizer that takes a while to eat. Try edamame (salted soybeans still in the pod), hot soup, or slippery seaweed salad. You'll fill up slowly and be less likely to shovel sushi in your face the second it arrives.

✳ Save calories by asking your sushi chef to go easy on the rice. Save calories (and fat) by asking the chef to go easy on the mayo in your spicy rolls.

✳ Slow down your eating by upping the spice factor. Mix a generous portion of that hot wasabi into your soy sauce and it'll be tough to overeat before the fullness factor kicks in.

✳ Befriend your sushi chef! It'll make it easier to custom-order your "light-on-the-rice, no-mayo, extra-crab" California roll. Who knows—he might even name a roll after you!

handy-dandy chinese food survival guide

Break out the chopsticks and break open the fortune cookies. It's time for Chinese food.

✳ Hungry Girl Hints

Master mealtime, whether takeout or tableside . . .

* Stick With It—Hate to use chopsticks because you have trouble eating with them? That's exactly why you should use these tricky sticks. Fiddling with them will force you to eat slowly.

* Get Steamy—Order your dishes steamed, with sauce on the side. Then dip, don't pour!

* Veggie Victory—A Chinese restaurant is one place you can always count on for delicious freshly steamed veggies—without even a drop of fatty oil or butter. Take advantage and order a side of 'em in place of rice.

* Brown Is Better—If you're going to eat rice, make it brown—not white. Brown rice is an excellent source of dietary fiber. White rice is an excellent source of empty calories.

● ● ● ● ● ● ● ● ● ● ● ● ● ●

Best Bets!

These low-calorie dishes rate high with us . . .

Steamed Veggie Dumplings (300 calories and 8g fat)

Buddha's Feast (200 calories and 1.5g fat)

Moo Goo Gai Pan (400 calories and 10g fat)

Steamed Shrimp and Broccoli (200 calories and 2.5g fat)

Nutritional information based on averages for typical serving sizes.

HG SHOCKER!

If your dish is swimming in thick sauce, just that gooey stuff alone will account for 200 to 300 calories and 5 to 20 grams of fat in your meal! Do yourself a favor—order it on the side, and use sparingly!

✳ Chinese Food Dos and Don'ts . . .

DO kick off your Chinese chowfest with a little soup. The average small serving of egg drop, wonton, or hot and sour soup will only add about 100 calories to your meal, and it'll help fill you up, too.

DON'T indulge in those fried chow mein noodles or wonton crisps restaurants serve by the basket. They add tons of fat and calories to an otherwise healthy meal. Ask your waiter not to bring any to the table or just place them out of reach on the other side.

DO avoid dishes that are breaded, fried, or coated in flour. That stuff does more than weigh down your plate. It'll weigh YOU down, too!

DON'T think all veggies are your friends. Broccoli trees are really good at sucking up and holding on to oil and fatty sauces. Eeeks (stupid trees)!

✳ Chew the Right Thing!

BITE IT! With just 25 fat-free calories, a fortune cookie is an awesome way to end your meal. And feel free to eat those orange segments many restaurants serve up, too. Your entire Chinese dessert will have less than 60 calories and practically no fat at all!

FIGHT IT! Those crazy almond cookies have about 85 calories and 5 grams of fat. They don't even taste that good. And have you seen that horrific oil spot those cookies leave on anything they touch? Gross!

mini italian food survival guide

You CAN survive a trip to your favorite Italian restaurant. Here's how . . .

✳ Dos and Don'ts of Dining Italia

DO start your meal off with a salad (light Italian dressing or oil and vinegar on the side) or some minestrone soup.

DON'T be afraid to request any of the seafood and poultry options grilled dry, with a heaping side of veggies. Then season those vegetables with a splash of lemon juice or balsamic vinegar, or dip 'em in a side of marinara.

DO eat bread *or* pasta, just not both. In Italy, it is a no-no to eat bread and pasta at the same time. Just skip the butter (who needs it when you have warm crusty Italian bread!), and stick with tomato-based sauce on your noodles.

DON'T order fish topped with cheese. Nix the cheese and you'll save calories and fat grams.

DO enjoy a bowl of fresh berries instead of some crazy, too-rich dessert.

DON'T clear your plate. It's okay to take some home with you to enjoy the next day.

DO ask for whole wheat pasta. Many restaurants (including the massive Olive Garden chain) offer up the fiber-rich stuff as a filling alternative to plain white pasta.

✳ Chew the Right Thing!

BITE IT! The average ½-cup serving of marinara sauce has about 95 calories and 3 grams of fat.

FIGHT IT! A ½-cup portion of classic Alfredo sauce has an average of 240 calories and 22 grams of fat!

Nutritional information based on dinner portions.

* *

✳ Chew the Right Thing!

BITE IT! A serving of Italian sorbet will only set you back about 150 calories, and it's fat-free. Or bite into a small almond biscotti for only about 100 calories and 3.5 grams of fat.

FIGHT IT! If you order tiramisu at an Italian eatery, your dessert plate will be packing about 1,100 calories and 60 grams of fat!

* *

HG HONORS!

Seek out these impressive Italian eats . . .

* Steamed Mussels or Clams, average (150 calories, 3g fat)

* Pollo Magro "Skinny Chicken," Romano's Macaroni Grill (330 calories, 5g fat)

* Spaghetti with Mushroom and Meat Sauces, The Old Spaghetti Factory (460 calories, 6g fat)

* Pesce Marinara (Fish in Tomato Sauce), average (400 calories, 8g fat)

* Venetian Apricot Chicken, Olive Garden (448 calories, 11g fat)

Nutritional information based on dinner portions.

pequeño mexican food survival guide

Don't let a trip to your #1 Mexican eatery get the best of you. Here's how to tackle a craving for Mexican, HG style . . .

✴ TOP ATE Taco-tastic Tips

1. Bulk up your meal with a side salad, or a side of veggies or beans.

2. Just say no to tortilla bowls, tortilla strips, guacamole, sour cream, and cheese.

3. Order two soft tacos, but eat only ONE tortilla. Just stuff what's inside the second one into the first and toss the extra tortilla. Your single super-stuffed soft taco will save you dozens of calories.

4. Avoid chimichangas, chalupas, enchiladas, and quesadillas—these are all fried and/or loaded with cheese.

5. Use salsa in place of dressing on your salads.

6. Take advantage of all the low-cal stuff like cilantro, jalapeños, and assorted chili sauces. You'll feel more satisfied if your meal is packed with flavor.

7. Order chicken or shrimp fajitas prepared without any oil. Then swap all the sides for a bowl of lettuce topped with tomatoes and a side of salsa. You'll wind up with a salad full of grilled veggies and more!

8. Avoid the chips at all costs (calories and fat rack up WAY too quickly).

On the Side . . .

Nutritional information based on averages.

✷ TOP ATE Diet-Friendly Mexican Food Staples

1. **Grilled Chicken**

2. **Shredded Lettuce**

3. **Jalapeño Peppers**

4. **Pico de Gallo**

5. **Salsa**

6. **Fajita-Style Veggies (grilled without oil)**

7. **Black Beans**

8. **Grilled Shrimp (no butter!)**

one-stop survival guide for road trips, airplanes, and cruises

Traveling isn't an excuse to shovel lots of bad-for-you foods down your gullet. Here's how to take a trip without taking a vacation from eating right . . .

✷ Snacks on a Plane

Relying on in-flight options for guilt-free grub isn't your best-laid plan. Here are some quick Dos and Don'ts for flying the friendly skies . . .

DO avoid the snack boxes with pretzels, crackers, and chips. Most of those snack packs have 600 to 900 calories and dozens of fat grams each. That's hardly a snack!

DON'T forget to do your homework. Check out your flight information online and find out what snack packs will be available to you.

DO stay busy. Bring magazines, handheld games, crossword puzzles, or even just a pen 'n paper to doodle on or to jot down some thoughts. By keeping your mind busy, you'll keep your appetite in check.

DON'T eat all of your emergency snacks on one flight (unless it's a true emergency—like the plane's been circling the runway for 18 hours!).

DO stay hydrated. Dehydration can cause grogginess and make it difficult to make smart decisions (like choosing to eat that apple you packed rather than those chips being passed around!).

DON'T underestimate your travel time. Factor in getting to the airport, waiting in line, and picking up baggage—even a short flight could mean many hours before your next meal.

HG's Guilt-Free Jet-Set Snack Pack

Pick one item in each category and create the perfect snack pack for about 300 calories . . .

* **Something Fruity**—Start with your favorite produce pick. Just remember to pack some napkins for those sticky-sweet selections.

* **Something Crunchy**—100 Calorie Packs and pre-popped single servings of low-fat popcorn are great airplane eats. They're filling, satisfying, and crunchy-good fun!

* **Something Protein-Packed**—A single-serving can of tuna (look for the ones with the easy-open lids), some jerky (beef, soy, or turkey), and light string cheese are all great ways to keep hunger at bay when you're airborne.

* **Something to Savor**—Low-calorie hard candies, lollipops, sugar-free gum are all awesome low-cal ways to keep your mouth busy. Plus, they'll protect your ears during takeoff and landing!

HG In-Flight Tip!

Take advantage of the "free to walk about the cabin" part of your trip. Stretch your limbs, stroll the aisles, and keep your blood flowing. You'll be less likely to munch mindlessly if you're alert and aren't achy. Happy travels!

★ Hit the Road, Jack!

Road trips can be a pain in the butt, and not just because you're literally sitting on it for hours. Face it—rest-stop food, fast food, convenience-store food, and gas-station fare are all fairly frightening. The trick is to bring on-the-go, easy-to-pack, guilt-free snacks to keep you fueled between meals or to use as meal replacements. Here are HG's Top 10 snacks to stash when you travel (in no particular order) . . .

1. Snack Bars
2. Instant Miso Soup Packets
3. Rice Cakes and Soy Crisps
4. Single-Serving 94% Fat-Free Microwave Popcorn
5. Low-Calorie Hard Candies
6. Instant Oatmeal Packets
7. Turkey, Soy, or Beef Jerky
8. Sliced Fruits and Veggies
9. Light String Cheese
10. Portion-Controlled Snacks (like 100 Calorie Packs)

. . . .

HG's Quick Road-Trip Fixes for "On the Go" Snack Options
So you forgot to plan ahead. No worries . . .

* Stop at the corner market instead of the corner fast food joint, and you'll have hundreds of healthy options.

* Take part in a Slurpee-fest at 7-Eleven, but only with the reduced-calorie Crystal Light Slurpees (which come in several fruity-licious flavors).

* Dying for ice cream? Who needs that awful convenience-store freezer loaded with bad choices? McDonald's has soft-serve, reduced-fat vanilla ice cream cones with just 150 calories and 3.5 grams of fat each. Well worth it!

* Frap Attack! There are Starbucks locations on practically every block in the U.S. (sometimes two per block!), so it's good to know that you can stop in and enjoy a Frappuccino Light Blended Coffee if you're craving a sweet blended coffee drink. Most are super-low in fat and have just 140 to 180 calories for a Grande size. Go for it!

Cruise Control

Eating is definitely a major part of a cruise. And all the rumors are true—there are usually multiple buffets at all times of the day (and night). But this isn't necessarily a bad thing . . .

* Embrace the Buffet—Buffets are packed with healthy options, and each one is a great opportunity to custom-build your perfect meal. Look for omelette stations (egg whites, no oil, and tons of veggies!), shrimp cocktail, cut-up veggies, fresh fruit, salad bars, and more.

* Drink Up—If cocktails are part of your celebration style, no worries! For low-cal cocktail choices, your best bottled bets are wine or light beer. For mixed drinks, stick with ones made with calorie-free mixers (like diet soda or seltzer) and then flavor them with all the fruit garnishes you can get your hands on.

* Speak Up—Cruise crews are used to special requests. The kitchen staff is usually prepared to cater to diabetics, vegetarians, and more, so if you want to special order something for the sit-down dinner, it shouldn't be a problem. Ask in advance to give them plenty of time to prep.

* Stay Active—Participating in physical activity on board is a great way to avoid feeling the effects of extra food. Most ships have fitness rooms, but even splashing around in the pool or playing shuffleboard on the Lido Deck burns calories.

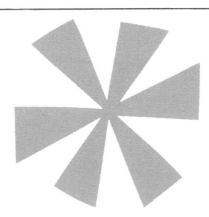

save-the-day office survival guide

Chances are you spend roughly 40 waking hours a week faced with tempting, diet-busting foods while you're at work. Don't be a victim! Arm yourself with the information (and snacks) you need . . .

✶ Office Dos and Don'ts . . .

DO avoid the kitchen. Keep utensils and a can opener in your desk, so you don't have to head to the kitchen for those items.

DON'T forget to plan ahead. Special-order lunches for meetings in advance. Or bring your own lunch if you can't special-order.

DO arm yourself with snacks. Make sure you keep your office packed with good-for-you treats.

DON'T snack from the vending machine. Even items that seem healthy (like trail mix or juice drinks) usually aren't low in calories.

DON'T wait too long to order dinner if you're working late. If you do, chances are you'll be too hungry to care what you're shoveling in your mouth.

The (Dreaded) Kitchen/Break Room

Conquer cravings in shared spaces . . .

HG Dilemma!

Does Susie in Accounting demand Potluck Pastry Fridays? Don't fall victim to the donuts and bagels that call out at you as you get your morning coffee. Get your coffee either *before* all the goodies arrive or after they've been picked over. Better yet, bring your own coffee from home and keep low-calorie sweets in your office for those weak moments.

EAT IT! Fruit, veggies, snack bars, cereal, yogurt.

BEAT IT! Cakes, cookies, bagels, donuts, muffins.

✴ Caffeine-y Meanies!

Don't break up the day with some sort of humongous, fat-filled, blended, whipped-cream-topped "coffee" beverage. The calories in beverages *count* (no matter what Maureen in Marketing tells you) . . .

SIP IT! Coffee, unsweetened tea, Starbucks Frappuccino Light Blended Coffee drinks, diet soda, sugar-free energy drinks.

SKIP IT! UBBs (Unidentified Blended Beverages), sweet tea, regular soda, sugary energy drinks.

USE IT! Fat-free and/or sugar-free non-dairy coffee creamer, no-calorie sweetener, sugar-free syrup, light soymilk, fat-free milk, fat-free whipped topping.

LOSE IT! Half & half, sugar, sugary syrups, cream, regular milk, whipped cream.

For more coffee tips, check out our Caffeine-Fix-in-a-Flash Survival Guide on page 314.

✱ TOP ATE Must-Have Office Snacks (No Refrigeration Required)

1. Canned Soups—If you're watching your sodium intake, keep an eye out for low-sodium versions because some canned soups are salty!

2. 100 Calorie Packs—You get the perfect snack-sized portion of whatever it is you crave—salty, sweet, chocolatey . . . you name it. Impressive!

3. Nut Mixes—Break these down into single-serving portions so you don't swallow the whole bag at once. The healthy protein and fat will keep you full for hours.

4. Fiber One Bars—There are about a zillion snack bars out there to choose from, but Fiber One Chewy Bars are the best ones to have around during those moments of candy-bar-craving desperation.

5. Tuna Pouches—Protein is the most satisfying of all food groups. Go at that tuna with just a fork, or break out some high-fiber crackers to top with the stuff.

6. Instant Oatmeal—It's low-fat, low in calories, filling, and easy to stash (it takes up less space than a couple of envelopes). Just watch out for a few of the crazy flavors that are packed with excess calories and fat grams.

7. Beef, Soy, or Turkey Jerky Snacks—Keeping a bag or two of this stuff in your desk is a great idea. It's low in fat and calories and packed with protein. Wanna know what's in HG's desk drawer? Tillamook Country Smoked Beef Nuggets.

8. 94% Fat-Free Microwave Popcorn Mini Bags—Fresh, delicious, warm popcorn anytime. And they even come in flavors like butter and kettle corn. You may want to occasionally pop up a multiple-serving bag. Your office mates will come running when they smell corn popping!

✴ TOP ATE Must-Have Office Snacks (If You Have a Fridge/Freezer)

1. Sugar-Free Gelatin and Pudding Snacks—These prepackaged, single-serving snacks have been faves of dieters for years.

2. Fat-Free Yogurt—Fat-free yogurt is an almost perfect food. It's nutritious and delicious.

3. Fresh Fruit and Veggies—There's no alternative to good old fruit and vegetables. They're crunchy, refreshing, great-tasting, and so good for you.

4. Guilt-Free Chilled Beverages—Whether it's water, diet soda, iced tea, or sugar-free lemonade, keep the fridge stocked with super sippers!

5. Sugar-Free Ice Pops—Stick a few in that tiny freezer compartment. You won't be sorry!

6. Lean Turkey Slices—Plain and simple, protein is good. Turkey slices are delicious. Eat them alone, with mustard, pickles, and/or Dijonnaise. You can even roll all that up in a few pieces of Romaine lettuce for a quickie protein wrap.

7. Fat-Free Cheese Slices—For those times when you are starving and need something you can pop in your trap quickly—but gum or sugar-free candy isn't gonna do the trick. Wrap your chompers around some cheddar, American, mozzarella, or Swiss.

8. Vitalicious VitaTops (vitalicious.com)—Each one of these muffin tops contains just 100 calories and lots of fiber. Always keep a spare one stashed in the freezer for emergencies. They ROCK!

Catered Meetings

Pay attention—it's okay to pull the cheese out from your sandwich, wipe the mayo off your bread, or even ask ahead of time to special-order your meal. It's all right to be high maintenance every now and then . . .

BITE IT! Lean deli meats, whole wheat bread, salad (dressing on the side), veggies, fruit salad.

FIGHT IT! Pre-made sandwiches, dressing-doused salad, pasta salad, pastries.

Desk-Bound Lunch-Hour Power

* Whenever possible, brown bag it. That way you're in complete control of your afternoon intake.

* If you do go down the takeout road, remember to special order. Ask for mixed greens or fruit instead of fries or pasta salad, and order all sauces and dressings on the side.

* Fast Food Friends—Subway's 6-inch subs with 6 grams of fat or less, Taco Bell's Fresco Style menu, Wendy's chili and baked potatoes, Panera Bread's You Pick Two menu (go for their low-fat soups, light salad dressings, lower-carb breads, and lean deli meats), Burger King's TENDERGRILL Chicken and BK Veggie Burger.

* Fast Food Foes—Oversized burgers and subs, taco salads in the shell, French fries, fried fish sandwiches, chicken nuggets, shakes.

Workday Birthdays—Take the Cake

If you show up in the conference room and announce that you aren't having any cake, you can be sure you will be hassled and berated until you're forced to eat a sugary slice, while everyone stares at you. Instead, take a piece, celebrate with everyone, and have a bite or two. Then fiddle with it, put it down, and slip out of the room. Reward yourself later with a small, sweet snack in your office—like a lollipop. Or squash the craving for cake altogether by popping a mint or chewing on some intensely flavored gum.

HG Tip! Browse through chapter 4 for ways to burn calories at work!

super-convenient convenience-store survival guide

Convenience stores can be convenient for everything except your diet. Here's how to get in and out FAST— with snacks that won't break the calorie bank.

The Inconvenient Truth

✳ Convenience stores are all about fatty, starchy, calorie-packed foods. Steer clear of any "meal" that is prepackaged. Those pre-made sandwiches are typically slathered with mayo, cheese, and other fatty extras. And those cellophane-wrapped bagels that come slathered in huge amounts of butter or cream cheese can contain 500+ calories and enormous amounts of fat. Eeek!

✳ Don't think for a second that a muffin is a better choice than a donut or even a greasy loaded breakfast sandwich. Muffins can contain 400 to 700 calories and as much as 30 grams of fat. With stats like those, you might as well have a hot fudge sundae for breakfast! (HG Note: That is NOT a recommendation to eat ice cream for breakfast.)

✳ Beware of the condiment bar. Chili, nacho cheese, and mayo are the condiment bar's worst offenders. If you need a condiment fix, go for the ketchup, chopped onions, mustard, or relish. They'll add taste without the extra fat and calories.

✳ If you must have soda, make sure it's diet. And, unless you're running a marathon, get a 12-ouncer. No normal human needs 52 ounces of artificially sweetened chemicals.

✳ Can't imagine a summer without Slurpees? There are several low-cal options to choose from. Look for Crystal Light and diet soda Slurpees, and save the 240+ calories in the regular ones for things you can actually chew.

✳ Stopping in for your morning coffee? Those cappuccino and hot cocoa machines are pumping out tons of calories. Go for flavored coffee (virtually calorie-free) instead. Then add some no-calorie sweetener and fat-free milk. Some stores even stock those yummy sugar-free (and calorie-free) flavored syrups. Yes!

✷ TOP ATE Convenience-Store Staples That Won't Wreck Your Diet

1. Fresh Fruit

2. Hard-Boiled Eggs

3. Light String Cheese

4. Light Yogurt

5. Baked Chips or Soy Crisps

6. Carrot Sticks

7. Lean Deli Meats

8. Mini Cereal Boxes

I WANT CANDY!

Most convenience stores are a good place to find retro candy. These candies may not be healthy, but they're fat-free and fairly low in calories. And they're certainly better than a lot of the other foods around. Treat yourself to one of these classics every once in a while.

✳ Jawbreakers ✳ Pop Rocks ✳ Blow Pops ✳ Ring Pops ✳
✳ Red Hots ✳ Lemonheads ✳ Atomic Fireballs ✳ Runts ✳
✳ Smarties ✳ Pez ✳ Pixy Sticks ✳ Razzles ✳ Fun Dip ✳

teeny-tiny guide to cocktail parties, holidays, and bbqs

People often use holidays and parties as excuses to eat poorly. Don't do it! Be cautious and deliberate about what you eat. There are a few simple things you can do to avoid going absolutely CRAZY at food-filled fiestas . . .

✴ The Dos and Don'ts of a Successful HG Party-Goer

DO opt for simple foods packed with protein and fiber. That way you'll be less likely to overeat (and even if you do, it's on healthy stuff). Shrimp cocktail, crudités (sliced raw veggies), and grilled chicken or beef skewers are great party staples to stick with.

DON'T indulge in anything shiny, cheesy, or fried. That means no mayo-soaked sides, oily appetizers, fatty dips, or deep-fried items. Macaroni salad, antipasto, artichoke dip, and popcorn shrimp are all crazy-high in fat and calories.

DO treat yourself to dessert. Load up on fruit salad and savor a few bites of your favorite dessert (so you don't feel deprived and wind up stopping for a carton of ice cream the minute you leave the party).

DON'T fall victim to those giant bowls of mixed nuts. Though nuts are healthy, it's much too easy to munch on them mindlessly and end up gobbling 'em up by the handful. And each pile you grab will probably have 150 to 200 calories and 15 or more grams of fat.

DO *check out more of our party tips on page 153.*

✳ Chew the Right Thing!

The 411 on hors d'oeuvres . . .

BITE IT! Assorted chilled seafood is an awesome option—shrimp, crabmeat, mussels, and scallops are all super-low in calories and fat. And you can never go wrong with fresh veggies, as long as you ditch the creamy dips and eat them plain or with a little salsa.

FIGHT IT! Pigs in a blanket (those cute little bundled-up hot dogs) have about 75 calories each. Little quiches and fried dumplings can easily pack in over 150 calories a pop (eeeks!). And a single stuffed mushroom or bacon-wrapped scallop can contain 65 big ones!

· ·

TOP ATE Tips for Guilt-Free Party Sips

No, you don't need to stick to water. Here are HG's favorite party sipper tips that allow you to skip the excess calories. Bottoms up . . .

1. If you're craving a mixed drink, choose one with seltzer or diet soda (calorie-free mixers = your friend) and a single shot of liquor, like vodka or rum. Then your whole drink will only run you about 100 calories.

2. Avoid fancy-schmancy frozen drinks like daiquiris, margaritas, and piña coladas. Those can easily contain 500 calories each!

3. Skip creamy liqueurs for sure. Those can contain insanely high amounts of calories and fat.

4. Don't be fooled by juice-based mixed drinks. Cranberry, orange, apple, and grapefruit juices can all add 50 to 75 calories to your cocktail. If you've gotta have a fruity fix, go with half juice and half seltzer.

5. If beer's your thing, go with light beer and save about 50 calories per drink.

6. Remember that tonic water isn't sugar-free or calorie-free. Choose diet tonic or seltzer instead.

7. Wine is low in calories—about 120 calories for an average serving—and it's easy to make one glass last. Save even more calories by drinking a wine spritzer (a few ounces of wine mixed with seltzer). Yum!

8. Remember, everyone loves a designated driver. No shame in skipping the cocktails and treating yourself to a little more of the party food!

Holiday HOT List!

Choose these guilt-free goodies at your next holiday party . . .

* Shrimp cocktail (4 jumbo shrimp w/1 tablespoon cocktail sauce = 75 calories and 1g fat)

* Hot holiday-blend tea (1 mug w/ no sugar = 0 calories and 0g fat)

* Candy canes (1 cane = 60 calories and 0g fat)

* Chicken or beef skewers (1 skewer = 100 calories and 3g fat)

* Raw veggies with salsa (1 cup veggies w/¼ cup salsa = 55 calories and <0.5g fat)

Nutritional information based on averages.

Holiday NOT List!

Don't overindulge on these holiday diet busters . . .

* Eggnog (1 cup = 400 calories and 20g fat!)

* Hot cocoa (1 cup w/whipped cream = 200 calories and 10g fat!)

* Assorted chocolates (3 pieces = 200 calories and 11g fat!)

* Cookies (1 chocolate chip cookie = 210 calories and 13g fat!)

* Cake (1 small slice of chocolate cake = 340 calories and 14g fat!)

Nutritional information based on averages.

• •

✶ BBQ Foods: INDULGE or AVOID?

EAT IT! Grilled chicken breast, turkey dogs or turkey burgers (often low in calories and fat, but read the labels if you can!), grilled veggies, corn on the cob, watermelon, fruit bars, and ice pops.

BEAT IT! Fried chicken, beef burgers, hot dogs, oily marinated veggies, potato salad, pasta salad, pie, ice cream (cones, bars, or otherwise).

USE IT! Lettuce wraps, mustard, ketchup, pickles, salsa, hot sauce, lemon juice, light salad dressings.

LOSE IT! Giant buns, cheese, mayo, BBQ sauce (or use sparingly), butter, full-fat salad dressings.

BBQ Shockers!

* The average BBQ meal contains 3,500 calories! That's at least 1,500 more calories than the average person should have in an entire day.

* In 2001, Americans consumed 7 billion hot dogs between Memorial Day and Labor Day alone (and we doubt they've lightened up in recent years)! That's a collective 2,205,000,000,000 calories!

* One serving of BBQ pork ribs delivers an average of 68 grams of fat and 1,360 calories! FYI, it'd take nearly 6 HOURS of post-BBQ cleanup to burn off all those calories!

reel deal movies survival guide

Eating at movie theaters can be bad news. There simply aren't very many good choices available there. Follow these easy steps to avoid becoming a DOUBLE FEATURE!

✷ Theater Dos and Don'ts

DO sneak your own candy into the theater. It's as simple as throwing some long-lasting, low-cal candy in your purse (lollipops, chewy stuff, and hard candies will last you long into the plotline!).

DON'T buy king-sized movie candy, even the fat-free kind, unless you're going to share it with a KING-SIZED group of friends! That 8-ounce bag of Reese's Pieces tips the scales with close to 1,200 calories and 60 grams of fat, and even that 6-ounce Twizzlers pack contains more than 550 calories. YEESH!

DO smuggle in a pre-popped mini bag of 94% fat-free microwave popcorn. Just pop it up right before you leave the house!

DON'T, under any circumstances, indulge in movie theater popcorn! A small container has about 400 calories and 25 grams of fat . . . WITHOUT BUTTER! A large container *with* butter packs in about 1,500 calories and 130 grams of fat. That's scarier than any horror flick to ever hit the silver screen.

DO stick to diet soda or water and save yourself from the sugary, empty calories in regular soda—a 40-ounce soda contains more than 500 calories! If you crave flavored liquid, bring along sugar-free powdered drink mix packets to toss into your water bottle.

DON'T think you have to forgo carb-y goodness altogether if you didn't pre-pop your own corn. Go for a warm and doughy soft pretzel (a medium one has about 350 calories and only 3.5 grams of fat) and share it with a pal. Just be sure your twisted treat isn't drenched in butter, cheese, cinnamon and sugar, chocolate, or any other crazy toppings.

Two Thumbs Up!

Sour Patch Kids and Lemonheads are fat-free and satisfying, yet not quite as addictive as other candies 'cuz of their sourness. HG Tip: Give away the green and yellow Sour Patch Kids (or whatever your least fave flavors are!) to pals sitting near you—that way, you won't eat those once all the good flavors are gone.

Pop To It!

Enjoying a movie-thon at home? With so many awesome options, you can really go to town! (Not literally. You can stay home and eat them.)

＊ **Jolly Time, Orville Redenbacher's, and Pop Secret all make 94% fat-free microwave popcorn in single-serving bags that contain only about 110 calories and about 2 grams of fat. Plus, each bag pops up a generous 5 to 6 cups of the stuff!**

＊ **LesserEvil's all-natural, fancy Kettle Corns (lesserevil.com) will knock your popcorn-lovin' socks off. They come in craaaazy flavors like Peanut Butter & Choco and MaplePecan. Each cup of the stuff will cost you 120 calories and 2 grams of fat. Not bad at all for such a decadent popped treat.**

＊ **Jolly Time's Healthy Pop Caramel Apple Microwave Pop Corn combines the sticky sweetness of caramel with apple-y fun to make completely guilt-free, flavor-packed popcorn—all for just 110 calories and 2 grams of fat per 5-cup serving! Woohoo!**

caffeine-fix-in-a-flash survival guide

Coffee was originally used for medicinal purposes, treating everything from heart disease to fevers and coughs. It wasn't until people started craving the caffeine-buzz "side effect" that coffee took on the hot beverage form we know and love today. But coffee isn't just COFFEE anymore. It's often buried beneath sugar, syrups, milk, and whipped cream. Here's how to have a fun coffee break without downing a gazillion calories.

✴ TOP ATE Ways to Survive a Trip to Starbucks

1. Always order your drinks "Nonfat" and "No Whip."

2. Tempted by those Frappuccino Blended Coffee drinks that come in a zillion crazy-delicious flavor combinations? They're ALL available as Frappuccino Lights, most with just about 150 calories and hardly any fat for a 16-ounce Grande.

3. If you order a flavored coffee, make sure the flavor comes from the actual coffee grounds as opposed to added sugary syrups.

4. Remember that "reduced-fat" pastries aren't necessarily low in calories or fat. (You're better off avoiding cake-y items altogether.)

5. Lose the idea that anything with "tea" in its name is diet-friendly. It's not.

6. Order a "Short" size drink (it's not on the menu, but your friendly neighborhood barista will happily accommodate you) if you want to indulge without going overboard.

7. Skip regular syrups, full-fat milk and cream, and sugar. Always opt for sugar-free syrups, fat-free milk, and no-calorie sweetener.

8. For guilt-free tea, order a plain unsweetened iced tea, then ask for a shot of sugar-free syrup and use no-calorie sweetener to flavor it.

✷ Chew the Right Thing!

How well do you know the creamer crew?

BITE IT! If liquid Coffee-mate (or liquid creamer, in general) is your thing, stick with Coffee-mate's Original Fat Free (1 tablespoon has just 10 calories). When looking for flavored coffee-enhancers, hit up the powders, in either Fat Free or Sugar Free. While they often SEEM to have more calories than the liquid, it takes FAR less of the powder to make your drink taste good (typically a teaspoon is all it takes). And a teaspoon of the stuff only adds about 10 calories or so to your beverage.

FIGHT IT! Avoiding regular flavored creamers (ones that aren't fat-free or sugar-free) is pretty much a given. But know that even the fat-free flavored liquid Coffee-mates have TWICE the calories of the Original Fat Free. Each tablespoon of the flavored liquids has about 25 calories. The sugar-free ones are no bargain either, with 15 to 30 calories and at least 1 gram of fat per tablespoon. That may not sound like a lot, but liquid creamers aren't nearly as potent as powdered ones. So it's way too easy to add 100 calories and even several grams of fat to your drink without even thinking!

· ·

Extra, Extra!
Skip these little extras to keep your drink from turning into a liquid fright-fest . . .

Whipped Cream Catastrophe—That big, scary squirt of whipped cream can add as much as 130 calories and 12 grams of fat to your drink. What a silly idea that is!

Syrup Downer—Each pump of those flavored syrups adds 20 to 40 calories to your beverage. The good news? The sugar-free syrups are calorie-free. Weeeee!

✶ Brew It Yourself!

To make awesome coffee drinks at home or at the office, have these HG-approved ingredients in your pantry at all times . . .

Instant Coffee—It does the trick in a pinch.

Unsweetened Cocoa—Adds chocolatey-good flavor with very few calories. Stick with a teaspoon at a time (about 5 calories) and use a no-calorie sweetener to bring out the flavor.

Light Vanilla Soymilk—Okay, this actually goes in the fridge. But it's a lifesaver.

No-Calorie Sweetener Packets—Whether you favor the pink packs, the blue babies, or (HG's fave) the yellow Splenda ones, keeping a stash of these on hand is key to creating coffee magic!

Torani Sugar Free Syrups—There are other brands out there, but Torani is the best, hands down. Their Almond Roca, Coconut, and Vanilla flavors are the best for coffee beverages.

Malted Milk Powder—Just one 10-calorie teaspoon adds a HUGE amount of maltiness to drinks.

Coffee-mate Powdered Creamers (Sugar Free or Fat Free)—SF Vanilla Caramel and FF French Vanilla are the best, and they have just about 10 calories per tasty teaspoon.

No-Caffeine Zone

Can't have lots of caffeine? There are TONS of ways to fulfill your coffee craving without going against the doctor's orders. Starbucks usually has two decaf coffees available on any given day—the house blend as well as a yummy flavored one. You can enjoy almost anything on the menu, practically caffeine-free, as long as you start with one of their decaf coffees. Just look out for other caffeine-laced ingredients (like an espresso shot) before ordering. Most other coffee chains will also make their classic menu items with decaf coffee.

Well, as sad as it is, like all good things, this book must come to an end. It's time for you to stop poking around here, anyhow, and head into the kitchen to start whipping up some guilt-free eats. This book was *so* much fun to write (I have to admit, the recipe testing was my favorite part!) and I hope it helps you realize that eating better is *not* about depriving yourself. You can easily find ways to eat the foods you love (even the so-called "bad" ones!) by whipping up fun and easy, better-for-you versions right at home.

Stay in touch—and please send your comments, feedback, and suggestions to me at hgbooks@hungry-girl.com. And for more recipes, news, food finds, tips, and tricks, sign up for our free daily emails at hungry-girl.com. *HG out!*

Index